Ready for Enlightenment?

An Insider's Guide to
the Biggest Trip of Your Life.

By Lex Sisney

LuLu
North Carolina, USA.

Copyright 2006 by Lex Sisney

Cover art by Kevin Milden.

All rights reserved. No part of this book may be reproduced or transmitted in any form or by any means, electronic or mechanical, including photocopying, recording, or by any information storage and retrieval system, without permission in writing from the publisher.

Published by LuLu, Inc.

North Carolina, USA.

ISBN 978-1-4303-2962-6

www.lexsisney.com

It's the year 2000. I'm 30 years old. My life is imploding. No one knows this yet. Not even me.

I play it cool. Heck, just look at me. Don't I look like I have it all together?

I'll just work harder, faster, longer… just like I always have.

I'll think positive and everything will work out in the end. You'll see.

I tell myself these things.

But that's not how it goes.

Not this time…

To Shanna. My wife and guru.

"Not only does *Ready for Enlightenment?* ring with truth and resonate with love, it is often as thrilling as an adventure story. If you are on the journey of greater spiritual awareness and conscious living, you'll find a wise friend and fellow adventurer in these pages. Enjoy!"

- **Gay Hendricks, Ph.D.**
  Author (with Dr. Kathlyn Hendricks) of *Conscious Loving* and *Spirit-Centered Relationships*. Co-founder, Spiritual Cinema Circle and Transformational Book Club

"Every now and then an authentic new voice arrives that embodies the essential truth of all wisdom traditions and literally communicates powerfully with every word. I found *Ready for Enlightenment?* stimulating, inspiring, and even though I am a veteran self-evolver, the book set me onward with some new goals, insights and specific teachings to learn from. Lex is so engaging, and having worked with him personally, I know what a remarkable teacher of transformation he truly is. I highly recommend this book."

- **Barbara Marx Hubbard, Ph.D.**
  Author, *Conscious Evolution: Awakening the Power of our Social Potential*. President, Foundation for Conscious Evolution

"Lex has written a guide to spiritual transformation in an elegant and straight forward way. I recommend this book to anyone interested in conscious evolution."

- **Deepak Chopra, M.D.**
  Author, *How to Know God*. Founder, the Chopra Center for Well-Being

"Lex probes the questions and longings felt by every sentient being. His insights are fresh and his metaphors are engaging. Most importantly, his zeal for life, awareness and reality flows out of every page and into the soul of the reader."

- **Jim Warner**
  Author, *Aspirations of Greatness*. Founder, OnCourse International

Contents

Preface — 9
The Call to Transformation — 11
What is Enlightenment? — 39
Ask — 61
Commit — 75
Practice — 101
Surrender — 133
Putting It All Together — 147
I of the Storm — 159
Appendix — 167
   Summary of the Steps to Awakening — 167
   Review of Key Questions — 169
   Resources for Your Trip — 174
   References and Further Reading — 181
   About the Author — 185

Preface

This is a book about an amazing and seemingly miraculous journey. It's the big trip, the great adventure to something indescribable. It's what we all want, even if we don't know it yet. It's the journey to enlightenment. You don't have to travel far to get there. In fact, you are already there. But making the trip requires courage, persistence, and dedication. It's also helpful to have a guide. Within the pages of this book you'll find a very simple, useable framework to make great leaps in your own conscious awareness and experience the lasting freedom, bliss, and happiness that goes with it.

There are just a few things to know before beginning. First, the book doesn't recommend a certain spiritual path or discipline. It honors all traditions, all paths, and all practices that point the way to one ultimate destination. Second, my desire is to provide a transparent look into the joys and trials of waking up, what to expect while you're transforming, and how to make the most of the process. Third, it's free of dogma and religiosity. The world doesn't need more doctrine. Pluralism, genuine sharing, and an open dialogue are the way forward now.

An elder member of the Arizona-based Hopi Nation recently gave this address. He captures the essence of what I wish this book to represent:

"To my fellow swimmers:

"There is a river flowing now very fast. It is so great and swift that there are those who will be afraid, who will try to hold on to the shore; they are being torn apart and will suffer greatly. Know that the river has its destination. The elders say we must let go of the shore, push off into the middle of the river and keep our heads above water.

"And I say 'See who is there with you and celebrate.' At this time in history, we are to take nothing personally, least of all ourselves, for the moment we do, our spiritual growth and journey come to a halt.

"The time of the lone wolf is over. Gather yourselves. Banish the word 'struggle' from your attitude and vocabulary. All that we do now must be done in a sacred manner and in celebration. For we are the ones we have been waiting for."

Your journey will be exquisite and it will be your own. But we're all in the river together. My wish is that sharing my own experience will help you in some small way, as others have helped me, on your own route to higher levels of consciousness. Together, we can share and celebrate the journey and help one another keep our heads above water. Collectively, we can contribute to something grand and wonderful... a consciousness of humanity swimming free. So are you ready for enlightenment? Turn the page and let's find out.

The Call to Transformation

"There is more to life than increasing its speed."

--Mahatma Gandhi.

How do you know you're ready for enlightenment--or at least more enlightenment? It's easy. You're in a crisis. Some*thing* or some*one* or some*how* is breaking down and causing grief and misery in your life. Plain and simple, life isn't working. You want it to change. But you're at a loss for what to do. All of your old tricks, tools, and methods to cope with life just don't seem to cut it any longer.

Imagine for a moment how you might react if your entire life seemed to be crumbling. As if all of the things you deeply valued in life seemed to be slipping inexorably away. And the things you used to cope with life's challenges--your management of time, money, relationships, thoughts, emotions, goals, dreams, work ethic, diet, exercise, faith, everything--it all just seemed to stop functioning like it used to.

Well, if you're like me (and most humans) the first thing you do is try harder. Do more. Re-commit. Knuckle down. Do it better. You do more of what's always worked for you before.

But what if that didn't seem to cut it either? What would you do then? It's quite a sticky situation.

I was as surprised as anyone to find that this quandary is exactly what happened to me. For most of my life, I had subscribed to a deeply ingrained formula for success. It sounded something like this: "set goals, think positive, work hard, be persistent, and you will achieve your goals." Does this tune sound familiar to you? It should. It's a set of beliefs so deeply ingrained in our culture that they're practically invisible: set goals, think positive, work hard, and you too can own the big house, drive the nice car, and have the fat bank account. It's the success formula for our times. You can find similar (if not identical) assertions in innumerable books, articles, and on the lips of coaches, teachers, mentors, speakers, and parents in all walks of life.

Does it work? Sure. But only up to a limited level of success. It's missing a key ingredient: *how to manage the accelerating change caused by success.*

In order to explain what I mean, allow me to share a little bit of my life story. When I was 10 years old, I made a big sign I hung over my bedroom mirror that said 'If I work harder than anyone else, I can accomplish anything.' Since I viewed myself as a shy, skinny, and awkward kid, my early goals were to transform my physical body. By high school, after lots of time in the weight room and on the track, I had become the captain of the football and track teams, set a school weight lifting record, and soon earned a black belt in karate.

Then, in my 20s, my goals shifted towards education and business. I paid my way through college and found out--which was news to me--that I was actually quite smart and a good student. My dream to travel and work in Asia manifested itself when I received a scholarship, an internship, and then a full-fledged career to do just that.

And by the age of 29 it seemed like the pieces of my life were coming together rather nicely. I had co-founded a business that was soaring like a rocket--in fact; it was one of the fastest growing private firms in the country. I had a six-figure income and a net worth of several million dollars. As the CEO I was fully able to express my creativity, passion, and vision in my career. The adrenaline rush was exhilarating and addicting. I was recently married to the woman I loved and we would soon have our first child. My health was good. We took exciting trips around the world. You get the basic idea.

I believed, and had proven to myself in my own small way, that the success formula of "set goals, think positive, work hard, be persistent" really did work to get more of what I wanted in life.

But fast-forward a few short years later: My life and dreams are disintegrating before my eyes. I can't blame it on anything tabloid worthy such as drug addiction, affairs, criminal activity, divorce, etc. Nope. On the surface I was doing everything "right"--setting goals, taking care of myself, focusing on what really matters, managing my time, working out, eating well, reading, meditating, asking for support, trying my best, working hard, being persistent. You name it. I was doing it.

None of it seemed to make much of a difference. It felt like my life was imploding on itself. No matter what I did to try to control things around me, it felt like it all was crashing down around my head. My marriage was frayed. My job was on the outs. My health was poor. Underneath a cool and calm veneer, I felt distracted, irritated, agitated, and perplexed. What was going on?

It was a subtle thing to notice at first. I call it the dilemma of success. With each level of achievement, I had grown beyond wanting just one thing, such as a successful career, so I added more things. I now wanted a successful marriage too, one based on love, commitment, trust and intimacy. Then of course after our daughter was born, to be a successful parent, a parent who would lead by example, be present, kind, aware, loving, and do the right thing for his children. I wasn't trying to live up to some societal expectation like Ozzie and Harriet, but from an inherent desire to be and do my best. Of course I wanted to be healthy, vibrant, and attractive too. I had a growing desire to develop my spirituality. I wanted more fun, more joy, and more true friendships. I wanted more time and more money so that I could learn, grow, and experience life to its fullest. And I wanted greater meaning in my life and to make a positive difference in the world. More, more, more. In essence, just like you, I wanted it all.

It was kind of funny in a way. I could spot everything I wanted in life coming together and slipping away at the same time. The more "big wants" I added, the more difficult it all became to keep together. It was like I was trying to keep five balls in the air at once. Sure, I could use goal-setting, positive thinking, persistence, and hard work to focus on one or two areas really well but when I did that the other areas would drop out of control. I could focus on my job but only at the expense of my marriage. I could spend time playing with the kids but only at the cost of my to-do list. I felt like I was being pulled in five directions at the same time, that no matter what I did, it wasn't enough. The more things I added, the more things fell apart.

You would never have known these feelings existed by looking at me or speaking with me. To outward appearances, I seemed happy, successful, together. But inside (although I wasn't quite conscious of this at the time) there was an underlying simmering of restlessness and dissatisfaction in my life. I had a constant inner dialogue going: "Just keep doing what you're doing, but do it better, faster, smarter." I tried to convince myself that once I hit "X" milestone or "Y" date that everything would finally come into balance. I could exhale. Finally, I would have "made it." The only trouble was that X and Y never seemed to get satisfied. Simply by trying to manage my life like I always had, but now at an accelerating and expanding scale, my life was falling apart.

The signs of disintegration were very subtle. None shouted out, "You've got to change your life. Now!" Rather, they were cumulative and insidious. Imagine a skyscraper built on a shallow foundation. The building looks strong on the outside, like nothing could topple it. But underneath the surface its foundation is slowly crumbling. One day a strong wind blows in and… boom! Looking back on that period in my life it is clear to me that I was on a path to destroy much of what I love. I was running so hard and so fast to "make it" that I was at risk of wrecking everything good in my life along the way. I just barely escaped being toppled by a strong wind.

For example, when I came home to spend time with my family, I would be physically present but mentally absent, thinking about something still on my task list. I would play on the floor with my baby daughter but my mind would be miles away. I was missing out on the fleeting moments of my life while I was living them. I was a grumpy grouch when I wasn't working. I was a grumpy grouch when I was working, but always underneath a cool and positive veneer. I put on 35 lbs. I was riddled with hidden anxieties.

Unconsciously, I sought solace from this inner turmoil and anxiety. So in my "down time" I would gravitate towards the readily available distractions of modern life--television, junk food, sexual fantasies, pornography, alcohol, shopping, surfing the Web. I'd use them to numb out and try to escape my inner turmoil. I'd tell myself that I was just "taking a break."

But even when I tried to tune out, part of my over-active brain would be reprimanding: "You're wasting time! Let's go!" Or even, "Is this the extent of your life? Loser!" My need to numb out would soon turn to guilt for having done so and then I'd get angry with myself, usually lashing out at my wife to boot, and out of guilt would work even harder. My life was like a set of instructions on a shampoo bottle: Work hard. Numb out. Feel Guilty. Express Anger. Repeat.

Of course my intentions were noble. I was trying soooo hard. Just as you do, I held a deep and committed desire to be and do my best--to be a good and better <u>insert your noun of choice here</u> (person, leader, executive, husband, father, friend, listener, citizen, contributor, whatever). But wanting and working hard at something wasn't enough for me to keep it together and deliver on my conscious and unconscious expectations.

I followed the classic success formula as best I could; set goals, stay focused, rise early, read, think, plan, exercise, build my network, manage my time, do my thing. I'd fall off course temporarily and then scramble back into place. "Let's go! You can do it! Keep it together! Bigger! Better! Faster! More!"

I convinced myself that I was doing it all for others--for my family, my co-workers, my shareholders. I was doing it for everyone else but me. "Look at how hard I'm working for you?" "Can't you people see how hard I'm really trying?" "Do you think I like working this late?" It was all bullshit. I was doing it all for *me*. I was driven by unknown and unrealized inner fears. I just didn't want to admit to it.

All in all, my experience of life implosion wasn't pretty, it sure wasn't any fun, but isn't it just so typical today? The volume of prescription drugs, stress related diseases, physical and verbal abuse, and general fear, unease, and unhappiness that is visibly present and increasing around the world today tells me that barely controlled implosion is pretty much standard living in today's "modern" world. As Carl Jung once said, "The greatest affliction affecting mankind isn't serious mental illness, but the general uneasiness and unhappiness that is so prevalent in our society." Spot on.

A turning point occurred for me when I was deep into a business plan for what would be my third entrepreneurial venture in six years. Why was I writing another business plan with all of this implosion stuff going on? Because I was afraid of change. Who wants to change? No one does. Like I said, when things aren't working well, we tend to first go back to what worked for us before. It's human nature. So that's what I was doing. I had convinced myself that I would do the next venture bigger, better, faster than the last time, thus solving all of my problems. Ha!

I had just finished the market analysis and defined the opportunity. The plan was good. It addressed a growing market need and I was beginning to see how all the pieces could fit together. But as I sat thinking and writing at my desk, I was overcome with a feeling of total despair.

I heard my own voice silently ask…

"Lex, what in the hell are you doing? … Your life is stretched and frayed to the max…. You have a new baby daughter… Your passion level should be at a 12 and it's at a -2… So whom are you trying to kid and why are you really pursuing it?"

"I don't know," I replied out loud as I hung my head in my hands.

Later on I would realize that that moment was a life-changing catalyst for me. Like fissures in a dyke that don't reveal themselves until the water pressure is severe, the paradigm of set-goals, think positive, work hard, be persistent, and everything will work out in the end, began to visibly reveal its cracks. I was miserable. I was unhappy. I had no idea why or what to do about it.

Pushing the business plan I was working on aside, I stood up from my desk and walked outside to clear my head. I had an epiphany: Under sufficient pressure, change, and scale, the classic model for success that had got me where I was just doesn't cut it. Change is a constant. That no matter what I did, it was never going to be enough. I could run has hard as I wanted but I would never "make it." In fact, the harder I ran one way, the more everything else would fall apart. Here's why:

Creating the life we want is really about creating the positive change we desire. We all desire more of something… more love, money, happiness, safety, security, worthiness, success, satisfaction, etc. But not only that, we also try to control and mitigate negative change from occurring… we all want less fear, loss, shame, illness, poverty, failure, unhappiness, etc. We're in a constant battle to accent the positive and control the negative. It's a never-ending battle because we don't live in a vacuum. The force of change is a constant in the Universe.

What's the problem with change? Nothing and everything, all at once. *Nothing* is wrong with change because change is perpetual. There's nothing we can do about it. It's always happening. It will always happen. It just is. *Everything* is wrong with it because change causes disintegration. It causes things to fall apart.

Just as a gently flowing Colorado River slowly disintegrates earth and rock over time to create the Grand Canyon, when change moves slowly it causes slow and steady corrosion. But even when the change is slow and subtle the total effect is still awe-inspiring. And when a fast moving tsunami strikes, instantly consuming an entire city, it's easy to see how rapid change causes rapid disintegration. Change causes deterioration. Slow change causes things to fall apart more slowly. Fast change causes things to fall apart more quickly.

Because change causes things to fall apart, we're always attempting to cope with it. We attempt to control things just as they are. We seek to accentuate the positive and stop or mitigate the negative. All of our actions and motivations in life can be viewed as an attempt to manage change towards our own perceived best interests.

Are your political views conservative or liberal? It depends on the change you want to see happen and your belief in which party can deliver it.

Perhaps you are apathetic about politics? Then you have little belief that any political party can steer the positive change you desire or halt the negative.

Are you healthy and fit? Then you will seek to maintain or manage your current state of well-being and prevent change.

Are you sick and frail? If so, and if you have the energy and capability, you will naturally seek out ways to make yourself well (i.e. cope with change).

The entire struggle of human existence summed up in a simple picture:

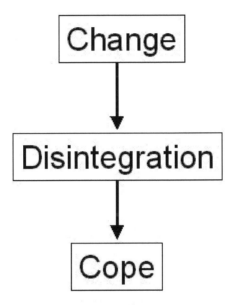

Figure 1. Change is a constant. We seek to manage it as best we can.

Change is a constant. It causes things to fall apart. We attempt to cope with the fallout as best we can. We try to halt the negative and get more of the positive change we desire. But here's the kicker. When we implement solutions to cope with change, guess what happens? We create more change! This creates even faster disintegration that requires new solutions that causes even more rapid change and thus disintegration.

Even our best solutions cause other aspects of our lives to quickly fall apart. Any individual or collective solution we implement to manage change actually drives change faster and causes even greater disintegration. Yikes!

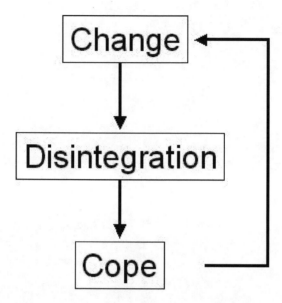

Figure 2. Whatever we do to cope with change creates more change.

We can easily see how this perpetual cycle works in our individual lives. Imagine that your business is expanding rapidly. Congratulations! This is something you've wanted for a long time and you've worked very hard at it. You've implemented a change management solution--business growth--to offset the disintegrating force of business failure. You're successful. Whew. But guess what happens next? Faced with the new growth, the businesses administrative systems and people are falling apart and must be managed to keep pace.

Of course this creates more change that must be managed. Since you've been working long and hard to advance your career, your family life is disintegrating and needs extra energy and effort to maintain. But when your family life is finally harmonious, your career has stalled and needs to be reinvigorated. With all the work, you've had to put off exercising and that paunch across your middle isn't so attractive. Since you're worn out and exhausted, your energy is weak and your diet is poor. So you get motivated and start a health kick. It's going well. You're running farther than ever but now your knees act up because they're deteriorating from the new change of running and need to be managed back to shape. You're forced to take it easy on your knees but now you just don't feel as fit any longer. On and on it goes. Is this life?

It's also easy to see how the change management fallacy plays itself out within society at large. A floodwall is built to protect a city. But the floodwall--yet another solution to cope with change--causes the destruction of local wetlands that in turn destroy the natural flood plain and provide less protection to the city.

Or one country wars with another to in effect, create change. War is yet another change management solution that causes rapid deterioration in the social fabric of both countries. This deterioration requires more coping strategies in an attempt to halt its spread and keep the social fabric together.

A media blitz is launched to convince citizens of the necessity for war. Diplomatic channels and refugee camps attempt to halt further disintegration but really just shift it to another domain. Now, there are refugees to deal with, sanctions, political diatribe, and the ongoing threat of future expanded war that causes additional disintegration that must be managed. On and on it continues. When the proverbial waters of change are high enough, disintegration happens dramatically and there's not much, if anything, we can do about it.

This cycle of "change--disintegration--cope--change" runs in a constant feedback loop. Individually or collectively, we undertake a vain attempt to control our world as we want it to be.

We are constantly striving to halt and mitigate the negative and to maintain and accentuate the positive. But every solution we implement causes other aspects of our life and society to fall apart. This causes us to climb back on the change management treadmill and run even faster to keep it all together. Despite our best efforts any solution is at best temporary and at worst accelerates larger problems.

With this epiphany, I began to understand that I was trying to run my life from the outside in, in a vain attempt to arrive. But everything I could achieve on the outside by the very nature of change would only come back to bite me in the ass. I was just trading activity for activity. Man, what a vicious cycle. It reminds me of an old Chinese proverb, "It is not wise for a blind man, riding a blind horse, to approach the edge of a deep pond." I was running so hard and so fast straight for the pond but I was blind to the reasons. What am I doing with my life? More importantly, *why* am I doing it? I began to take stock of my situation and what I saw didn't look very good.

I admitted to myself that the driving reason I was writing that new business plan was because the company I founded and was having so much satisfaction leading a few years ago had imploded too, just like me. And damn that was painful to admit.

Back in April 2000, I had closed a large, multimillion-dollar funding round just as the stock market began to collapse. Soon after came Sept. 11, 2001, followed by an even deeper economic recession. Despite these steep challenges, the team and I brought the company to cash flow profitability exactly three years to the month after we started the business.

Years later, the business has gone on to be quite successful grossing several hundred million dollars annually. But in the middle of all this, directional battles with the venture capitalists, painful layoffs, business model reinventions, and colossal mistakes on my part cost me my position as CEO. I was "promoted" to Chairman of the Board, where I could be kept safely out of the way. With the market tanked and preferential treatment assigned to the financiers, my net worth was in shambles and no big payday was in sight. Despite not knowing what I was going to do next, I told the board that I wanted out of the day-to-day business. My heart was no longer in it. They happily agreed. I was given a short severance. I was worried about money. What would I do after the severance ended?

My relationship with my wife was in a state of disrepair too. Stretched, frayed, tense. We just weren't getting along that easily. She blamed me for being constantly engaged elsewhere. I felt unsupported in my pursuits. Even playing with my daughter would only provide temporary relief from my pressure to "do something."

Taking a cold hard look at how my life was running then made me ask some tough questions. "Will I ever make it? Will I ever have enough? If I have all the money, recognition, and power I desire, will it really be enough?"

I wanted to say, "Yes! Just a little more, just one more time and I promise that will be enough." But inside I knew that was a lie. It would never be enough. Every goal and milestone I had hit in my life only provided temporary satisfaction and sometimes none at all. I knew that I would always keep moving the yardstick. There's no satisfaction in past achievements, no matter how great they may appear from the outside looking in.

"So what should I do?" I asked. "How can I just leap back into the fray with a new business? Wouldn't I lose everything if I did? Would it be worth it to end up with the gold ring of outward success and a lump of coal for the rest of my life? No thank you. There had to be a better way. But is there a better way?"

Dropping out and joining a monastery wasn't an option, neither was cutting back and seeking more simplicity. I didn't feel like I was overextended by my schedule itself, but rather by how I managed my thoughts and feelings within my schedule. Besides, I didn't want less from life, I wanted more.

A traditional church or religious organization wasn't it for me either. Anytime some person or entity purports to me, "this is the one true way" or "thou shalt not…" I cringe and flee. I'm too much of a free thinker for any kind of crappy dogma.

The idea of going on an anti-anxiety or anti-depression medication struck me as a cop-out. Besides, I was scared of the side effects. Although who knows, maybe I should've popped a few pills just to see?

But there were several things that did seem to make a somewhat positive difference in managing the tide of implosion and anxiety I was feeling in my life.

The first was a love of learning. I have always been a voracious reader (thanks Mom and Dad) of anything and everything I thought could be useful to my life. Over the years, I had cultivated a deep curiosity and love of exploration. I think what I love most about a book is the discovery of that one big idea that I can take away and try on in my life. In fact, I've never read a book that didn't have at least one interesting and useful concept in it.

But despite my joy of reading, I have always struggled with implementing consistent, real-time (or in the moment) application of the concepts from any book. For me, intellectual understanding was always overpowered by the visceral reaction I experience in the moment. If you have 150 e-mails to answer, 10 phone calls to make, and you're fighting with your spouse, how much good does the axiom "be one now" do for you? Very little I presume. So while I might get great insight from a book, I get no lasting comfort.

Another tool that seemed to really help was meditation. By the time I was writing that business plan and reached my turning point, I had been regularly meditating for two years. What originally led me to meditation was that I had recognized that the faster my external world went, the more active my internal mind became. Later on I would realize just the opposite… the faster my internal mind went the faster my external world appeared… but I'm getting ahead of myself.

With all the change and speed happening in my life, I took up meditation because I dearly wanted some quiet between my ears. The little I knew about meditation then was that it was a good tool to calm the mind and reduce stress.

But I also had a hunch that mediation would help me in other ways. My own experience showed me that all of my great insights and decisions never came from my analytical mind alone. Sure, I would think things through with my mind, but never once did I make a great decision or have a creative breakthrough using just intellectual analysis. Instead, if I was working on a new project at work or pondering what to do about this or that, the answer I sought would come flooding into me in those rare times my mind was quiet. Usually when I was in the shower, late at night, or while exercising. So in addition to quieting the chattering monkey between my ears, I reasoned that meditation might help me access more creativity and intuition too. And who wouldn't want more of that?

I found a meditation program in the Yellow Pages and signed up for a three-day course. Like everything else, I dove in with gusto. My initial goal was to meditate twice a day for 20 minutes each period. But the early results were the opposite of what I expected. Instead of experiencing my mind quieting down, my thoughts seemed to be speeding up.

I learned later that the typical human brain processes one to three thoughts per second--over 50,000 per day during our waking hours. That's a lot of thoughts; too many to consciously spot. So my mind actually *was* quieting down. I just had a terrifically larger number of thoughts than I was previously even conscious to. By meditating, I was slowing my brain down just enough to become more conscious of them.

I stuck with it. Every day, twice a day, I'd take time out from my busy schedule, sit down and meditate. My mental chatter finally did start to slow down. As I continued to meditate, I felt more inner peace and greater self-awareness from the practice. I also was accessing more intuition and creativity in my day-to-day living. More and more frequently I found myself instantly knowing something without being able to explain how I knew. I just knew. Hunches, insights, and creative inspiration became a more regular occurrence as the chatter in my head gave way to more stillness.

One other tool that seemed to help--at least temporarily--was personal development workshops. I began attending different versions of these in my late 20s. Where a book couldn't make the leap to real-time application, and meditation was a good all around practice, retreats and workshops gave me deep tastes of the inner peace I was seeking.

For instance, I was aware of the way subconscious conditioning I collected in childhood still strongly influenced my present day relationships. If you've ever found yourself repeating the same old fight with your lover or saying something that your father used to say, even though you vowed never to say it yourself, then you know exactly what I'm talking about. This unconscious conditioning--referred to as "patterns"--can unknowingly run, and very often ruin a life.

Before my wife and I got married, we each separately took a 10-day pattern-clearing workshop, followed later by a joint weeklong one, to help us clear out the personal baggage we each carried into the relationship. If you've never done a workshop like this, I highly recommend it. They can be incredibly revealing and transformative.

We also got into the habit of attending different relationship seminars on our anniversary. The accumulated soot of every day living can build up to mar an intimate relationship. We'd always debate going or not going; "What are we going to learn this time that we haven't learned already? Haven't we done enough of this stuff yet?"

But for many years, we'd go "just to see." I think we also went out of fear of not keeping our relationship together if we didn't make the commitment to it. After each event, we'd always share a laugh on the ride home because of how much personal gunk, up-to-then-unknown, we actually did uncover and transform. It was a good trade. We'd invest a weekend in our relationship and then get to enjoy reveling in newfound love and intimacy for many weeks and sometimes even months later. But over time, those feelings would wear off and we'd be back in that frayed, tense place I first spoke about.

Just like books and meditating, personal growth retreats also helped to mitigate my feelings of disintegration. Each, in their own way, provided a boost along the path but none seemed to provide a panacea for the stress and implosion of everyday living I was experiencing.

Despite only providing a boost, these early explorations into the practice of personal development had whetted my appetite for more. I originally took them up to get more performance and throughput in my life.

But something else magical was happening. I was learning more about what makes me tick and why I do what I do. I began to recognize a deeper part of me too. Someplace within that felt very *real* but until now had remained hidden. This place felt timeless, eternal, powerful, blissful, and all knowing in its scope. It certainly wasn't overwhelmed by anything happening in the outside world. It seemed to reside calmly beneath the roiling surface of my conscious thoughts and unconscious conditioning. By and by I came to understand this emerging sense within as my

Authentic Self. When I would stumble upon it, however briefly, I experienced transcendent moments of joy, bliss and oneness that significantly broadened my horizons about life and its possibilities.

I recall my first introduction to my Authentic Self exquisitely. A friend had recommended I attend a personal development workshop called the Hoffman Process in Napa Calif. At age 26, it was my first real foray into a workshop setting. I wasn't sure what to expect. My friend just said to go; that it would be the most challenging and rewarding thing I would ever do. Something about what my friend said just clicked for me and even though money was tight and I was in-between jobs, I paid for the workshop and a plane ticket and off I went.

The program was very intense, inwardly revealing, and totally fantastic. At one point, after exerting lots of effort to understand and release my biggest self-limiting obstacles, I was self-introduced to a part of me that I never new existed. I met my Authentic Self.

During a meditation, I came face-to-face with the inner me. Here I was, not a skin encapsulated ego defined by his activities and possessions but a powerful vortex of white light and indescribable energy. It was both searing in its heat but also heatless. It felt like pure love. Even though it was a meditation, the realness of it all was undeniable. In an instant of clarity, I finally understood what all those books I had read over the years were talking about. "Oh, that's what they meant by the Authentic Self! Ahh, now I see. It all makes so much sense now. Wow. Wow."

I got up from the meditation and walked outside still carrying elements of what I just witnessed. Every leaf and blade of grass had a never before seen vividness and light surrounding it. I felt one with everyone and everything in creation. Love came pouring out of me. I felt fearless, free, and liberated. This was my first taste. But the important thing is that it opened my horizons to a part of me that I never knew existed, but in reality was always there.

As I continued my early forays into personal transformation via reading, meditation, and workshops, I'd occasionally stumble into similar kinds of peak-like experiences. Cumulatively, I was experiencing dips into something incredible; first hand experiences of a deeper and more authentic part of me. Was there more there? Could I get more regular access to it?

I began to form a notion that if I could just integrate and anchor me within my Authentic Self more deeply then I could easily handle any feelings or signs of implosion in my life. I reasoned that if I *could* do that, then I would naturally be more present, make better decisions, attract more wealth, have more energy, enjoy improved relationships... you name it.

I was still determined to have all the outward success that I previously sought but now with lasting peace of mind. I began to look at my Authentic Self not as an abstract thing to access once in a while, but as the only practical way to get more of what I wanted. "Geez," I thought, "Here's a crazy idea. What if I could just turn my entire life over to this thing--this mysterious and seemingly all knowing all powerful place within me--that would be pretty cool, wouldn't it?"

An inner question started to form in my mind, "Can I realize myself more fully? Can I take the little self awareness I have and magnify it?" I wasn't certain then but it seemed like a worthwhile question to ponder and perhaps the only real path to truly having it all.

I began to call my little project "the calm cool dude at the center of the storm." My emerging vision was of this calm, centered Zen-like master. He was still totally involved with his business, marriage, children, community, but he was never controlled, controlling, or overwhelmed by those activities. Instead, he would just sit in the center of it all and effortlessly influence the ideal outcome. He was my ideal of a spiritually enlightened being who at the same time, was also completely engaged in the world.

    Using my Authentic Self as an anchor, I felt I could then be more aware, creative, capable, insightful, powerful, attractive… you name it. I would be more successful now and in the future. I had a hunch that I really could get it all in life by simply going deeper to a place within. I wanted to know more about that inner place and have more regular access to it. I started to articulate a new success formula. Rather than "set goals, think positive, work hard, and be persistent," my new success formula was forming to look like "discover and anchor myself within, find my true calling to serve, and turn the details over to the Universe." Wow. It was a really inspiring vision for me. It still is.

    So with no other road map at the time other than "to look within" I decided I would take some time off from my career--up to six months--and explore new methods and tools to manage my life from the inside out.

    The six months kept going and as I write this book, it's been nearly six years since. The journey absolutely has not been easy. In fact, it's been the hardest, most intense, and most gratifying work I've ever done and it never ends. The rewards so far have been priceless.

    Today, among other things, I am terrifically more productive, prosperous, engaged, contributing, and aware… all the things I originally wanted when it felt like my life was imploding. I just didn't get them from the classic outward model of success. I got them from my new inward model of true prosperity, one that delivers infinitely more than I ever thought possible when I began.

    I live life today almost totally from my Authentic Self-- that same timeless, infinite, secure, joyful, expansive, pure and real place that is you and that is within everything else. I still have unconscious moments when I forget my connection, but it is always there with me. I can always feel it. Sometimes it's in the background. More and more it's in the foreground and the centerpiece of everything I do and all that I am.

Words can't adequately describe the connection. At best they can point to it. How can you describe the taste of a pineapple to someone who's never tasted one? You can have all the scientific data and analysis on how pineapples are supposed to taste but until you've tasted one, you have no idea.

But on a practical level, my life feels guided. Everything in my life just falls perfectly into place without any struggle or effort on my part. I've transformed from running as fast as I could, stressed, worried, anxiety ridden, and hopelessly trying to control people and events to my satisfaction; to a new state of living filled with ease, flow, power, prosperity, creativity, and true bliss. I've gone from living in fear and trying to force my life to how I wanted it to be, to embodying love and powerfully co-creating my life as it's called to be.

And what about the classic success dilemma--the fact that change compounds change and causes things to fall apart ever faster? Actually, living life from your Authentic Self is the only way to counterbalance the disintegrative force of change. It acts as a cohesive force to keep everything together that should be together. It also provides unarguable clarity as to what to let go of and when. In fact, your Authentic Self is the only solid ground to stand on in a shifting, accelerating world.

Living life from your Authentic Self might sound like some abstract concept. It's not. It's as real as it gets. I've learned that it is the only practical way to truly have it all. Without it, success is empty: You can have the experiences and the possessions of success but they're laden with fear. Fear of losing. Fear of failure. Fear of what's next. You can experience pleasure and joy but they're short lived. You can run as fast and as far as your little legs will carry you but you're never going to make it.

Change begets change begets change. Things fall apart. Without the Authentic Self as an anchor you're running on an ever-speeding treadmill in a futile effort to try to control life as you want it to be. You're consumed by outward events and miss out on the true joy of moment-to-moment living.

But anchored within the Authentic Self, everything changes. Life takes on added dimensions of subtly and character. Success flows to you in all forms… health, love, joy, fulfillment, bliss, and prosperity. When I compare and contrast my old life with my new life led by my Authentic Self it's easy to spot the differences.

When I come home to spend time with my family, rather than being distracted and mentally unavailable, I am present and playful.

When I'm working, rather than worrying about "how to" do something, I just do what brings me joy and everything takes care of itself. New business opportunities, key relationships, and money just fall into my lap without any struggle or effort.

When I'm engaged in conversation, rather than an active chatter brain, my mind is still and I experience the essence of my conversation partner.

Instead of being sickly and overweight, I am healthy and weigh what I did as a junior in high school. I am overflowing with creative energy and vitality.

Often I'm overwhelmed with ecstatic feelings of joy, bliss, and oneness. They just sweep over me. I cry from the beauty of it all. I can consciously access more bliss at any time. It's all right there.

This is some of it. There's so much more. I can state unequivocally that the inner life is the answer to true success and prosperity and everything else you could possibly desire.

To be certain, I don't live this way all the time. Yet. I'm like an adolescent bird that's learned to fly but still has some downy feathers around its neck. Outward events still overwhelm me. I go unconscious. Old feelings of fear and control come back. I play out unconscious patterns.

But it's ever easier for me to spot when this happens. It's like a record player that hits a nasty scratch. Krcckkkkkkkkkkk, "Whoops, oh look at me, I've gone unconscious again." That's OK. I just keep learning and growing. I remember my connection and come back to the anchor of the Authentic Self. When I'm living there then life is miraculous. I wouldn't have thought it possible.

So how did I make this progression to an entirely new way of living? And what did I do during these six years? Actually, what I've done isn't nearly as interesting as what I haven't done.

I didn't drop out of society and join monastery. Nope, I stayed fully engaged with my life, my family, and the world.

I didn't travel to Tibet or India on a spiritual pilgrimage. Instead, I explored many different spiritual and personal development classes and workshops here at home. The same kinds of classes and workshops you can find in any independent newspaper or holistic living catalog in your city.

I didn't join a religion or follow a set-program. Rather I simply followed my heart and chose those things that seemed most interesting and beneficial to me at the time.

Does this sound trite? It should. These things anyone can do. People do them all the time. Heck, I was a seminar junky before my call to transformation. I was an avid reader and meditator too. As I said before, these things did seem to help at least a little bit to stem the tide of implosion in my life that I was feeling. But I was still imploding. I was still stressed, agitated, fearful, and missing out on the moments of my life. I was still struggling, confused, and living far less than my potential. So what made the difference this time?

It's this…. I chose it.

The essential idea here is this. My life was in a crisis. I allowed myself to open to change. I chose the inward journey as my path. At the start, I was simply seeking new tools and methods to do what I had always done, but do it better. I didn't want anything radical. I just wanted a few good tips and tools to get me back in the game.

But as I learned new things about myself, what makes me tick, and the path of transformation, my desire to grow kept expanding ever onward. One insight, one discovery led to another. My attention kept finding higher and higher ground as I sought ultimate answers. The question "How can I have it all *really*?" kept bubbling up into my consciousness. I followed that innate desire to have it all to its farthest logical conclusion.

In a process that I'll discuss throughout this book, I began to accept that the only lasting method for joy, prosperity, health, and happiness was self-realization. Piecemeal tools for stress release, meditation, manifestation, and self-understanding, no matter how good they might be, would forever fall short.

With this awareness my desires began to change. Rather than wanting to "do it better" I now desired to "turn it over" and live an entirely different kind of life. True self-realization became my highest goal. It's that simple. I chose it. I wanted it. I still choose it. I still want it. It's my only real desire. That's the secret to real transformation. We grow as fast and as far as we want to grow.

So if you take only one thing away from this book take this: ENLIGHTENMENT IS AS CLOSE AS YOU TRULY WANT IT TO BE.

You are already enlightened. Your Authentic Self is *you*. It is that timeless, eternal, powerful, creative, silent, still, and perfect part of you. It does not die. It does not feel pain. It is capable of moving mountains. When you truly want enlightenment then you're staking your God-given claim to remember who you really are. This is the secret; want lasting freedom more than you want anything else.

Wanting enlightenment isn't something you can just do casually. It's not an "Oh, sure. Enlightenment sounds really nice. I think I'll have some after my afternoon tennis match." It's not a part-time practice. On this trip, your spiritual growth isn't something you turn to on Sunday mornings or during your mediation. If you're ready to have it all then your Authentic Self must become the centerpiece of your entire life. You walk it, breathe it, practice it, and commit to it all the time in every moment. It becomes your ongoing, living reality.

I think there's a misconception on the spiritual path that desire is the root of all suffering. Not true. It's not attaining your desires that cause suffering. Desires are wonderful. They're an important aspect of being fully alive. Just choose them wisely. Choose your greatest desire as the highest goal possible, the full expression of you. Everything else flows naturally from that commitment.

It shouldn't be too surprising that desiring enlightenment, being fully committed to the process, is the key difference maker in your journey. You already have lots of evidence that desire and persistence is required to attain a goal in all other areas of your life. Let's do a quick exercise and see what I mean:

Recall some big and inspiring goal you've achieved in your life to date. Perhaps it was success in business, school, sports, or the arts. Pick something that you feel proud about accomplishing. Reflect on the process of attaining it.

First, notice how you really *wanted* it. You were committed to it. You made sacrifices in other areas of your life to get it. The degree that you wanted it mobilized all kinds of resources that you may not have even been aware of at the time. You overcame all kinds of obstacles. You realized new and amazing things about yourself. Finally, you achieved your goal or something even better.

In a nutshell, you followed the classic success formula to the letter: you chose a goal, thought positive, worked hard, and maintained persistence. Voila! Success!!

Irony of ironies, the journey to self-realization is essentially the same process. There are a few key differences that we'll explore in further chapters. Namely, your goals shift from "out there" to "within here" and at the ultimate step, you give up trying to have it your way all together and trust in your Authentic Self. But the essence of the journey is the same as any other goal you've already achieved in life. You've got to want it. Deeply commit to it. And dedicate your life to achieving it. There is no other method I know of.

The call to transformation happens through a crisis. I allowed my crisis to unfold into an astounding journey. I got everything I set out to get--plus much, much more--I just didn't get it in the way I thought I would. So if you're in a crisis, congratulations. This is your wake up call. It's time for transformation. It's the crises that provide the fuel, desire, and inspiration to evolve. Your innate desire for evolution--for lasting freedom, peace, bliss, prosperity and happiness gives you wings. Use them and fly.

Five questions to ponder regarding your call to transformation…

1. What's working really well in my life? What's not working so well?

2. What are the subtle, and not so subtle signs, pointing to potential disintegration?

3. If I could snap my fingers and transform anything in my life instantly, what would it be, what would I change?

4. Earlier in my life I experienced a call to transform. To take a new direction, go a new route, or discover something new about myself. When was it? What happened as a result? What were the ultimate benefits?

5. Whom do I know who has totally transformed themselves from the inside out? What was their experience? How does it relate to my own?

What is Enlightenment?

"Believe nothing because a wise man said it.
Believe nothing because it is generally held.
Believe nothing because it is written.
Believe nothing because it is said to be divine.
Believe nothing because someone else believes it.
But believe only what you yourself know to be true."
--The Buddha

As I began to ask myself, "Can I realize myself more fully?" some obvious follow-up questions began to emerge in my consciousness. Questions such as: "What is enlightenment anyway?" "I wonder what it would feel like?" "What are the benefits of having it or being it?" I acknowledged to myself that I didn't have the slightest idea. In fact, the whole notion was kind of unsettling to me.

As a young boy, the word "enlightenment" conjured up images of yogis living in mountaintop caves or stories of the saints of old. I imagined enlightenment as some kind of super-human state. A person who is self-realized must be fearless, powerful, holy, and perfect. Perhaps they even had the ability to create and cause miracles such as manifesting things out of thin air, walking on water, levitation, and other extraordinary feats. And surely, it must be that you could tell an enlightened person just by looking at them. They would have a glowing, golden aura and a beatific presence. In a way, they would be both awe inspiring and terrifying at the same time. That's what I figured as a little boy. By the age of the 30, my concept hadn't gone any farther than that little boy's imagination.

So what is enlightenment? My adult, rational mind suddenly needed to know. If you're planning a vacation, it's helpful to read up on the places you're going to travel before you leave home. Having a road map is a good idea too. With a map you have a better idea of what to expect along the way, where to turn, and when to stop. You can track your progress and recognize your final destination. Since I was considering the possibilities and potential of enlightenment, I wanted to know as much about it as I could. I wanted a brochure and a map.

The Wikipedia encyclopedia defines enlightenment as "the sense of any transformation into greater wisdom." I like that definition. It's simple and straightforward. But what kind of wisdom is it referring to? Is enlightenment a fixed state--does one somehow become enlightened and that's it, party's over, and you've made it? Or does enlightenment continue to evolve? And if so, then evolve to new levels of what? Can anyone attain enlightenment? Or does it come as a gift to the super-lucky or super-blessed?

The rational mind loves to analyze, judge, and label things. It's detailed, precise, and considers itself to be objective. Its playground is science and it demands proof, evidence, facts, and reason. Scientific research in all fields of human endeavor has made a dramatic improvement in our understanding of how many things work. Thankfully, the search to understand self-realization is no exception. It can be reassuring to know that enlightenment has been studied and quantified. It tells the rational mind that it's a normal part of living. In fact, all other living is abnormal.

Two key figures that have made a giant impact in our rational understanding of the path and experience of human evolution are the American psychologists Abraham Maslow and Clare Graves. By reviewing their work, we can gain a deeper understanding of human evolution, why it occurs, and what it means to experience higher states of self-realization.

Maslow (April 1, 1908 – June 8, 1970) was a brilliant theorist of human transformation. Maslow hypothesized that humans evolve through a hierarchy of needs. The primary human need is physical survival. When we are able to master our basic survival, we shift our focus to creating an environment that makes us feel safe and secure. When that's accomplished, our attention shifts to the need for belongingness and love. When we are able to master the art of relationship building, we shift our attention to satisfying our need for self-esteem. When we are able to feel a strong sense of self-worth, we shift the focus of our awareness to self-actualization or realizing our full potential.

Maslow represented this hierarchy as a pyramid. Beginning with the need for survival at the bottom and culminating with self-actualization at the top. We've all seen the original Maslow pyramid. It's usually shown as five levels like this:

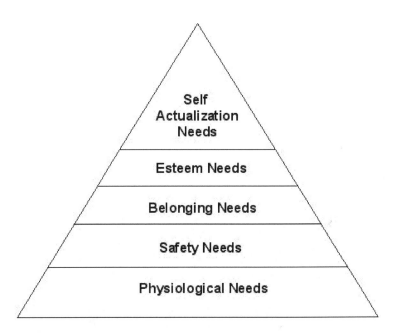

Figure 3. Maslow's incomplete pyramid.

When you look at this image, it seems like human evolution eventually stops. One gets to self-actualization and it's like you've hit a glass ceiling of transformation.

But strangely enough, Maslow didn't have just five levels to his pyramid. He actually had seven, two more than what is popularly known. Prior to the 1970 revision to his original 1954 pyramid in his book <u>Motivation and Personality</u>, Maslow added *above* the need for self-actualization the need to acquire knowledge and the need to understand that knowledge.

This "knowledge quest" doesn't emanate out of fear or to reduce anxiety of the unknown. Nor is it to acquire information to exploit an advantage. Rather, it is a natural extension of the pure joy of learning, curiosity, and growth. And at the very top of the pyramid was placed the aesthetic needs for beauty, balance, and structure. Maslow doesn't say much about this need other than to recognize that the impulse for beauty, structure, efficiency and completeness is found in every culture and in every age as far back as the cavemen.

Also not popularly known is that within the realm of self-actualization itself, Maslow actually identified two types of self-actualizers: "nontranscenders" and "transcenders."

Nontranscenders are healthy, well-adapted individuals. They have all of the characteristics of self-actualization--the internal, natural, drive to become the best person possible. Maslow describes the characteristics of self-actualization as follows:

> "...he has within him a pressure toward unity of personality, toward spontaneous expressiveness, toward full individuality and identity, toward seeing the truth rather than being blind, toward being creative, toward being good, and a lot else. That is, the human being is so constructed that he presses toward what most people would call good values, toward serenity, kindness, courage, honesty, love, unselfishness, and goodness."

Transcenders, on the other hand, share the exact same characteristics of self-actualization as nontranscenders but with one important addition. For transcenders, peak experiences or transcendent states of being become *the* most important things in their lives. Maslow found that transcenders undergoing peak experiences felt more integrated, more at one with the world, more in command of their own lives, more spontaneous, less aware of space and time, more perceptive, more self determined, and more playful.

> "Feelings of limitless horizons opening up to the vision, the feeling of being simultaneously more powerful and also more helpless than one ever was before, the feeling of ecstasy and wonder and awe, the loss of placement in time and space with, finally, the conviction that something extremely important and valuable had happened, so that the subject was to some extent transformed and strengthened even in his daily life by such experiences."

It's the transcenders who move beyond self-actualization into these higher realms of being that Maslow later identified. In his posthumously published work The Farther Reaches of Human Nature, Maslow describes and muses on the characteristics of self-actualized transcenders as follows:

1) They value peak experiences and plateau experiences above all else.

2) They speak easily, normally, naturally, and unconsciously the language of Being (B-Values), the languages of poets, mystics, seers, and profoundly religious. They better understand paradoxes, parables, figures of speech, music, art, and nonverbal communications.

3) They perceive the sacredness of all things at the same time that they also see them at the practical everyday level.

4) They are much more consciously and deliberately motivated by transcendent values of Being, perfection, truth, beauty, goodness, unity, and joy.

5) They seem somehow to recognize each other, and to come to almost instant intimacy and mutual understanding even upon first meeting.

6) They are more responsive to beauty.

7) They are more holistic about the world than are the nontranscenders. Mankind is one and the cosmos is one, and such concepts as the "national interest" or "the religion of my fathers" or "different grades of people or IQ" either cease to exist or are easily transcended.

8) They have a natural tendency to synergy that transcends the dichotomy between selfishness and unselfishness and includes them both under a super ordinate concept.

9) They more easily transcend the ego, the self, and the identity.

10) They are lovable, more awe-inspiring, more "unearthly", more "godlike", more "saintly" in the medieval sense, more easily revered, more "terrible" in the older sense.

11) They are apt to be innovators, discovers of the new, than are the nontranscenders, who are rather apt to do a very good job of what has to be done "in the world."

12) They can be more ecstatic, more rapturous, and experience greater heights of "happiness" (a too weak word) than the nontranscenders but can also be less "happy". They are maybe more prone to a kind of cosmic-sadness over the stupidity of people, their self-defeat, their blindness, their cruelty to each other, their shortsightedness.

13) They recognize that some things *are* better than others but also recognize the inherent beauty and worth in all things.

14) They show a strong correlation between increasing knowledge and increasing mystery and awe.

15) They are good selectors of people, despite appearances.

16) They are more "reconciled with evil" in the sense of understanding its occasional inevitability and necessity in the larger holistic sense. Since they have a better understanding of it, it generates both a greater

compassion with it and a less ambivalent and more unyielding fight against it.

17) They regard themselves as carriers of talent, instruments of the transpersonal, temporary custodians so to speak of a greater intelligence or skill or leadership or efficiency.

18) They are more apt to be profoundly "religious" or "spiritual".

19) They have a strong primary identity. They know who they are, where they are going, what they want, what they are good for, using themselves well and authentically in accordance with their own true nature.

20) They can be more childlike in wonder; fascinated by the colors in a puddle, or by raindrops dripping down a windowpane, or by the smoothness of skin, or the movements of a caterpillar.

21) They perceive everything as being miraculous and perfect just as it is.

22) They have a wholehearted and unconflicted love, acceptance and expressiveness rather than the usual mixture of love and hate or authority and power.

23) They value higher forms of payment beyond monetary reward. Money might still be important but higher forms of payment such as loving service and creative expression grow in increasing value.

Funny, Maslow found just as many self-actualized transcenders among businessmen, industrialists, managers, educators, and political people as he did among the professionally "religious" who are supposed to be transcenders and are officially labeled as so.

Clare Graves (Dec. 21, 1914--Jan. 3, 1986) was also a brilliant American psychologist. Graves took the hierarchical or "Level Theory" of human development originally proposed by Maslow to entirely new… well… levels.

Graves' key contribution is a theory, today called Spiral Dynamics, that "man's nature is not a set thing, that it is ever emergent, that it is an open system, and not a closed system." The essence of Spiral Dynamics theory is that as life conditions surrounding us change we, individually and collectively, develop new mental-emotional constructs to better cope with that change. In essence, it's change that drives human evolution. The more rapid and extreme the change, the more potential that exists for human evolution.

Graves' model, created using in depth research and analytical tools, shows how the evolution of an individual as well as the evolution of a group, community, society, country, and even a planet, follows the same evolutionary pattern.

Each level in the hierarchy alternates between an internal world view that occurs when a person is trying to make the external environment adapt to his or her self, or an external world view when they are adapting themselves to the external environment. This swing in focus between the internal and external world creates the cyclical or spiral aspect of his theory, hence Spiral Dynamics. Graves saw the process of evolution as a progression between relatively stable non-changing periods interspersed with unstable changing periods as never ending, up to the limits of the brain--something he viewed as far greater than we have yet imagined.

These evolutionary levels are not rigid but come in waves. According to Graves, each and every person has the *potential* to unlock every level of evolution. When you reach a new level, you embrace and transcend the old one. This creates much overlap and meshing between the waves.

In their book <u>Spiral Dynamics, Mastering Values, Leadership, and Change</u>, authors Don Beck and Christopher Cowa--who both worked actively with Graves--describe human development (so far) as proceeding through eight general stages, which are also called memes.

The word 'meme' in Spiral Dynamics is a play on the word 'gene.' Just as your genetic code influences and controls your physical body, your memetic code controls and influences your thoughts and emotions. When your meme is aligned with prevailing life conditions, everything is hunky-dory. But when your life conditions change, your primary meme needs to adapt too, otherwise you're going to suffer from unhappiness, struggle, and strife because there's a mismatch between your world model and the world itself.

Here's a brief overview of the eight general stages described by Beck and Cowan. The memes are given as color codes. Colors are used, rather than numbers, to reflect that no level is superior to another. They're just different. All levels are necessary. To experience healthy evolution, we need to integrate each meme before proceeding to the next one.

The first six colors of the Spiral represent the "old paradigm" memes for living and working and are called "Subsistence" memes. The last two, called Second Tier or "Being" memes, represent "new paradigm" memes for a *new era* of living and working that is emerging on earth now.

Beige

Survivalistic. Do what you must just to stay alive. Uses instincts and habits just to survive with a focus on food, water, warmth, sex, and safety. Distinct self is barely awakened or sustained. Forms into survival bands to perpetuate life.

Where seen: The first peoples, newborn infants, senile elderly, late-stage Alzheimer's victims, mentally ill street people, starving masses, bad drug trips, and "shell shock." Described in anthropological fiction like Jean Auel's Clan of the Cave Bear.

Purple

Magical. Thinking is animistic; magical spirits, good and bad, determine your results in life. Main purpose is to keep the spirits happy and the "tribe's" nest warm and safe. Form into ethnic tribes. Preserve sacred objects, places, events, and memories. Observe rites of passage, seasonal cycles, and tribal customs.

Where seen: Belief in guardian angles and Voodoo-like curses, blood oaths, ancient grudges, chanting and trance dancing, good luck charms, family rituals, and mystical ethnic beliefs and superstitions. Strong Third-World settings, gangs, athletic teams, and corporate "tribes."

Red

Impulsive. Be what you are and do what you want, regardless. The world is a jungle full of threats and predators. Breaks free from any domination or constraint to please self as self desires. Stands tall, expects attention, demands respect, and calls the shots. Enjoys self to the fullest right now without guilt or remorse. Conquers, out-foxes, and dominates other aggressive characters.

Where seen: The "Terrible Twos," rebellious youth, frontier mentalities, feudal kingdoms, James Bond villains, epic heroes, soldiers of fortune, "Papa" Picasso, wild rock stars, Atilla the Hun, William Golding's Lord of the Flies, and Mighty Morphin Power Rangers.

Blue

Purposeful. Life has meaning, direction, and purpose with predetermined outcomes decided by an all powerful Other or Order. One sacrifices self to the transcendent Cause, Truth, or righteous Pathway. The Order enforces a code of conduct based on external, absolute principles. Righteous living produces stability now and guarantees future reward. Impulsivity is controlled through guilt; everybody has their proper place. Laws, regulations, and discipline build character and moral fiber.

Where seen: Rev. Billy Graham, Frank Capra's *It's a Wonderful Life*, Puritan America, Confucian China, Hassidic Judaism, Dickensian England, Singapore discipline, codes of chivalry and honor, charitable good deeds, the Salvation Army, Islamic fundamentalism, Garrison Keillor's Lake Wobegon, Boy and Girl Scouts, patriotism.

Orange

Achievist. Act in your own self-interest by playing the game to win. Change and advancement are inherent within the scheme of things. Progress by learning nature's secrets and seeking out best solutions. Manipulate Earth's resources to create and spread the abundant good life. Optimistic, risk-taking, and self-reliant people deserve their success. Societies prosper through strategy, technology, and competitiveness.

Where seen: "Success" ministries, Ayn Rand's Atlas Shrugged, Wall Street, Rodeo Drive, The Riviera, emerging middle classes, the cosmetics industry, trophy hunting, chambers of commerce, colonialism, TV infomercials, the Cold War, DeBeers diamond cartel, breast implants, fashion, J.R. Ewing of *Dallas*.

Green

Communitarian. Seek peace within the inner self and explore, with others, the caring dimensions of community. The human spirit must be freed from greed, dogma, and divisiveness. Feelings, sensitivity, and caring supersede cold rationality. Spread the Earth's resources and opportunities equally among all. Reach decisions through reconciliation and consensus processes. Refresh spirituality, bring harmony, and enrich human development.

Where seen: John Lennon's music, Netherlands' idealism, Rogerian counseling, liberation theology, Doctors without Borders, Canadian health care, ACLU, World Council of Churches, sensitivity training, Boulder (Colorado), GreenPeace, Jimmy Carter, Dustin Hoffman in *The Graduate*, animal rights, deep ecology, Minneapolis-St. Paul social services, the music of Bruce Cogburn, Ben & Jerry's Ice Cream company.

From the green meme, it's possible to make an *exponential* leap in human evolution to the **Second Tier**. The primary difference in the second tier is that one can now appreciate all the different levels of evolution below. Before this ascent, when you're in one level of meme, you can't empathize with other memes. In fact, you're usually in conflict with them.

We see this conflict all the time in modern culture. Blue fundamentalism expresses disdain and hatred for green egalitarianism. Blues view the openness of greens as "sinful" and aggressively organize to fight against a further degradation of blue values in the media, politics, and commerce. Greens see the blues as mind controllers, exploiters of fear, violent, short-sighted, and hypocritical. In the first tier, neither side is yet capable of recognizing the necessity, need, and worth of the other. Both sides want the other to "become more like them."

Memes express themselves in individual personalities as well. An Orange entrepreneur is motivated by risk taking, winning, and keeping score with money and prestige. A Purple new ager seeks meaning and direction through mysticism in horoscopes, palm reading, and numerology. Orange judges Purple as woo-woo and Purple judges Orange as shallow and selfish. This inherent conflict between individuals and groups all changes at the second tier.

At the second tier you deeply appreciate and respect all the tiers below. You recognize that each level in the spiral is necessary for individuals and societies to evolve. After all, you can't reach the top of the stairs without all the preceding steps below. Here's a brief synopsis of the first two levels of the second tier.

Yellow

Integrative. Live fully and responsibly as what you are and learn to become. Life is a kaleidoscope of natural hierarchies, systems, and forms. The magnificence of existence is valued over material possessions. Flexibility, spontaneity, and functionality have the highest priority. Knowledge and competency should supersede rank, power, status. Differences can be integrated into interdependent, natural flows.

Where seen: Carl Sagan's astronomy, Peter Senge's organizations, Stephen Hawking's *Brief History of Time*, W. Edward Deming's objectives, Paul Newman's version of stardom, chaos theory, appropriate technology, eco-industrial parks (using each other's outflows as raw materials), early episodes of TV's *Northern Exposure*, Fel-Pro Inc. (a gasket manufacturer), Fred Alan Wolf's "new physics," Deepak Chopra's Ageless Body.

Turquoise

Holistic. Experience the wholeness of existence through mind and spirit. The world is a single, dynamic organism with its own collective mind. Self is both distinct and a blended part of a larger, compassionate whole. Everything connects to everything else in ecological alignments. Energy and information permeate the Earth's total environment. Holistic, intuitive thinking and cooperative actions are to be expected.

Where seen: Theories of David Bohm, McLuhan's "global village," Gregory Stock's *Metaman*, Rupert Sheldrake and morphic fields, Gandhi's ideas of pluralistic harmony, Ken Wilber's "Spectrum of Consciousness," James Lovelock's "Gaia hypothesis," Pierre Teilhard de Chardin's "noosphere."

     Beck and Cowan identify coral as the next emerging level in the Spiral but its theme and characteristic beliefs and actions were not yet clear to the authors.

     Evolving up the spiral is not a one-way trip. You can scale down the evolutionary spiral too. For example, another way to view my own life implosion is that my prevailing memetic code couldn't handle the changing life conditions I was experiencing. The rapid change in my life was causing my world model to crack open. When I eventually gave up trying to make things work the old way, I loosened my grip on my old memetic code and began the search for new answers and methods to better manage my life.

     By seeking out new methods, I began the process of moving up the evolutionary spiral to first understand and then integrate a more robust code to better match my new life conditions. But if I tried to continue on like I always had, or was unwilling to adapt, I would eventually fall backwards down the spiral to a previous memetic code that I had lived through earlier in life. We can move up the spiral of evolution, or down, depending on our capability, resources, and willingness to adapt to change in our environment. If we're afraid or unwilling to adapt, we'll spiral down in our evolution. If we are willing and able to adapt, we'll eventually spiral up. This movement up *or* down is true on an individual as well as planetary scale.

Comparing Maslow and Graves, we can see that a self-actualized person could actually be so at any level of the Spiral above the first color, beige, when self-awareness starts to happen. That is to say that depending on the time, place, and prevailing life conditions, a person could be a self-actualized purple, red, blue, orange, or green. We might call them a healthy blue or a healthy green person.

But it's self-actualized transcenders (Maslow) or Tier 2 individuals (Graves) that best seem to qualify for a rational discussion of what it means to be enlightened. Using Malsow and Grave's research as a reference point, we can gain some hints on the experience of what it's like to be enlightened. It's transcendent. It's transpersonal. It's evolving. It moves from a focus on the self, survival, and protection, up through a series of developmental stages in oscillating waves of inward and outward receptivity. The Spiral Dynamics group especially has gathered plenty of quantifiable research (a left brain favorite) that describes the condition of man at the base levels of existence and also infers what life might be like at the farther reaches of human nature.

It is reassuring to have a brochure and a road map of enlightenment. I think it helps to know that many others have had experiences of higher states of consciousness… even enough to actually measure their numbers and results. It also provides a description of an unfolding evolutionary process.

On the other hand, my need for rational understanding certainly never contributed to my happiness. In fact, the stronger my desire to intellectually "know-how-things-work," the heavier my mental burden became. At one point in my quest I had become a very sharp, intellectually penetrating machine that was also very arrogant, demanding, and a real know-it-all SOB. I was living life completely in my head disembodied from my heart. The need for sensible, workable answers on life's great questions is innate but it's a fine balance between the need to know enough and the need to know it all.

The fact is that a rational discussion of what it means to be enlightened is a little bit like the difference between reading a book about flying a plane and actually flying a plane. To understand what it means to be enlightened, we need to experience it firsthand. It's ancient wisdom and tradition that provide a rich history in how to do that.

There's a common theme among all wisdom traditions and across all cultures through history: In order to experience higher states of awareness, one has to go beyond rational thought. You can't think and analyze your way to enlightenment. You've got to transcend the thinking mind to get access to it.

When the rational mind is silent, even for a moment, a person begins to experience higher states of awareness. We've each had all-encompassing insights before. When they occur, they offer a glimpse behind the curtain of physical form. They seem to reveal a deeper reality or truth. They show what's possible in a way that our rational minds could never comprehend. An intuitive jolt can greatly aid in conceptualizing our understanding of higher states of consciousness. A taste can create memories that last a lifetime and it whets the appetite for more. We can get these intuitive hits at anytime, anywhere, and while engaged in any activity. They occur when we are fully present in the moment.

Nature, art, music, poetry, architecture, and beauty can all provide a doorway to higher levels of human perception. A sunrise, a painting, or a compelling piece of music can take our breath away and lift us beyond the ordinary. When it happens, we're overcome with a sense of perfection and humility. As the 14th century Persian poet Hafiz, a deeply spiritual seeker and lover of nature wrote, "I have estimated the influence of Reason upon

Love and found that it is like that of a raindrop upon the ocean, which makes one little mark upon the water's face and disappears."

Physical exercise such as yoga asanas, dancing, cardio vascular training, weight lifting, and sports of all kinds, can also provide transcendent feelings of being part of something large than yourself. As one ultra-marathoner, 135-mile foot race across the hottest desert in the United States, puts it "It was epic. I can't even explain it… It was very empowering, very life altering."

Meditation, contemplation, and prayer allow us to transcend the intellect and touch deeper levels of being. When we slip beyond the rational mind, we become more established in our essential state. As Lao Tzu, an ancient Chinese philosopher put it, "No thought, no action, no movement, total stillness: only thus can one manifest the true nature and law of things from within and unconsciously, and at last become one with heaven and earth."

Pyschotropic drugs such as peyote and psilocybin have been used for thousands of years to aid the opening of awareness. Just recently, in July 2006, the results of a study (an aid for the rational mind) on the effects of hallucinogens was reported by the popular media. Conducted by Johns Hopkins University, two-thirds of the volunteer participants who took a dose of psilocybin (otherwise known as "magic mushrooms") recounted a profound spiritual experience. The positive effects appeared to last for as long as a year.

Authentic creative expression provides a path. When you're totally absorbed in expressing a deeper part of your soul, doorways to higher realms begin to open up. Engrossing work, singing, loving sexual union, the joyful expression of innate talents, loving service, can all take you beyond the mundane to the heavens.

And of course the essence of all the world's religions also point the way to higher realms of being. In essence, a religion attempts to point the way to a deeper reality, a more profound truth that resides behind and within the world we can perceive with our senses. Any authentic religion points a way to realizing the truth of who you are; to find the reality of existence. Buddhism: "One who acts on truth is happy, in this world and beyond." Christianity: "You will know the truth and the truth will make you free." Hinduism: "The highest truth is reality distinguished from illusion." Devout practitioners of all religions can experience divinity, a knowingness of truth that can't be explained by the rational mind.

Infinite opportunities for greater knowingness and expansion exist everywhere. They occur when our rational mind is quiet and create a sense of what Maslow called peak experiences. On the journey to enlightenment, these little glimpses of "something more" begin to get more frequent until they make up an entirely new level of existence.

Both rational and intuitive methods for understanding enlightenment are accurate but also incomplete. The quest for self-realization is a personal endeavor and the only thing that really counts is your own direct experience. How are you feeling? Blissful? Ineffable? Joyous? Prosperous? Your truth is your truth and mine is mine. Neither can be validated by any external sources. Words fall woefully short of describing higher states of being. At best, they act as a signpost pointing towards an unknown land.

My direct experience tells me that I am not enlightened. I am *enlightening*. I am *realizing*. So are you. While you might experience an instant and permanent transformation, I certainly haven't. My journey has been one of progression. I began at one level of consciousness. At this level, I held a basic set of beliefs about God, about life, and about myself. I felt a certain way. As my journey progressed, I had blips and peeks into higher levels of consciousness. I opened up to new and higher realms. But these were only peeks. Soon after I would fall off. Many times I fell off below my base level of consciousness into states of despair. It was like I was given a taste of heaven but forced to wallow in hell. At one point, I surrendered and powered through these interminable, lower levels of consciousness to reside at an entirely new plateau. With this new plateau as a base, my journey of dips and progressions continued, albeit much smoother and within a much closer corollary than my old plateau.

Imagine a tall hotel. Viewed from a progression in consciousness, I began life living in the cheap rooms in the basement. I didn't know my room was in the basement. I didn't even know it was cheap. My room was my room. I had no context for other rooms. I had no visibility into the upper floors of the hotel. One day, the hotel manager knocked on my door and offered me a tour of the lobby and the nicer rooms in the main hotel. Wow, this was a pretty cool tour. I had no idea people lived in such opulence and grace. Here I was living in the basement, with just a small light in the ceiling and a cold hard bed. My tour out of the basement was both a blessing and a curse. It was a blessing because it opened my eyes. A curse because I couldn't afford to live in the higher, nicer rooms, yet and I was sent back to the basement.

Talk about depressing. But I had a vision of what was possible and this was all the motivation I needed to work hard, practice, and make my way to reside in the better rooms of the hotel permanently. Life in the nicer floors of the hotel became my new plateau. Occasionally, I'd get lost and wander down to the basement. I didn't like it there but I couldn't figure out how to get back to my new and better room right away either. Eventually, through grace or from the help of a kind and benevolent bellman, I'd get back to my nice room.

But one day, something miraculous happened. I was riding my usual route on the elevator between floors when, like the movie *Charlie and the Chocolate Factory*, it suddenly shot upwards out of the hotel with powerful force. When it finally stopped, the door chimed and I stepped off. I found myself in a strange but somehow familiar new hotel. This hotel was high in the clouds and connected by the elevator shaft to my old hotel below. I had heard fantastic rumors about such a hotel in the sky but they seemed far-fetched. Actually, they never did it justice. Life at this new hotel is a total blast. There are still variations in consciousness here. "Good" days and "bad" days happen. But nothing that occurs here is ever really overshadowed by the unbelievable view, the delicious food, the soul moving music, the fascinating guests, the world-class accommodations, and the brilliant service of this ineffable hotel. But even here, I've heard rumors of higher floors and better accommodations above. I can't even imagine. How do I get *there*?

What is life like at my current plateau? I feel life as *bliss*. That's the closest word I can come up with. It's an intimate and physical connection with what's real. On my good days, that connection extends and blends into everyone and everything in the Universe. I sense it as an ongoing and *unfolding* process of transformation. It's a journey that *uncovers* reality. I have gone from residing in my head most of my life to living from my heart most of the time. I mean this both figuratively and literally. Figuratively I'm transforming the fear and uncertainty of my intellect to the love and knowingness of my heart. Literally my sense of physical place in my body has also shifted from my head to my heart. It's a little different perspective but a far superior view.

My tastes of ecstatic living tell me that to be enlightened is to stand on solid ground between infinite paradoxes. I accept everything just as it is. I witness its inherent beauty. At the same time, I have a desire to improve things, to help make things even more beautiful, efficient, and whole. I am incredibly selfish... everything I do is for my own self interest. I choose to do things that make me feel good. To feel more blissful right now. And at the same time, I have a desire to serve, to teach, to heal, to give, to contribute. It's a refined sense of selfishness. I've gone from self-centered, concerned, and fearful about feeding, clothing, sexing, acquiring, exploiting things for my own advantage to a more Self-centered being with a desire to be happy by going within, seeing and accepting life as it is, serving and celebrating others, and experiencing great beauty and bliss. I can be filled with great love and also from love demonstrate great discipline, rage, and anger. I value physical life and at the same time, see the illusion of the physical world. I value peace and at the same time understand the role of war, horror, and atrocities. I am cosmically blissful and cosmically sad all at the same time. I see and cherish great good in the world. I see and accept great evil in the world. I am both yielding and infinitely solid. I am the same as everyone and everything and because of my vantage point, above the fray. I am one with God and at the same time I want to be well used by God. I have desires, I want to achieve my God-given mission and purpose and I am desireless, I am just as ready to leave the body and return home right now. I see and hold the superior point of view and recognize the value and perspective of all points of view. I am able to act with excellence in the modern world and at the same time, sit and do nothing as the Universe unfolds at my feet.

I want to scream out, "Wake up! Wake up! Wake up! There's a real party going on and I want all my friends to join me. Let's all wake up together! And the entire world will live in happiness and peace. Wake up!" And at the same time, I recognize that everything and everyone is absolutely perfect just as it is.

And what about my boy-hood visions of mountain top yogis and miraculous feats? While everything is possible, I haven't experienced anything like them myself. But when you're living in a state of bliss, total security, and loving service, what else really matters? Not much in my opinion. And it's clear from all the evidence, scientific, intuitive, and experiential, that this state is available to all of us. In fact, it's our natural state. So that leads us to the most important question: Can you realize more fully? Of course you can. You already know this to be true. You have changed and evolved in miraculous ways over the years. How far can you go? As far as you want.

In the following chapters I share the basic framework I used to make the leaps to entirely new levels of enlightenment as well as the joys and trials I've experienced along the way. Consider this framework like the blueprint of a house. You're building your dream house, I'm offering a blueprint you can use to build it quickly. It's a simple and flexible guide that anyone can follow to become more self-realized and live totally from your Authentic Self. It works with any path including a traditional one such as a religion, as well as for the "spiritual free agents" who prefer to mix and match different practices and even create new ones. It begins with the questions you ask, followed by your commitment, practice, and surrender.

These four things--Ask, Commit, Practice, and Surrender--build your experience of higher states of consciousness. As you read each chapter, look for the key accelerators that can jump your life to increased levels of bliss, happiness, prosperity, and guidance. Self-realization is the most fantastic and rewarding trip there is. Once you really get going, there's no way you'll ever want to turn back. Godspeed.

Five questions to ponder regarding your experience of enlightenment...

1. What is my most memorable transcendent, peak experience – my awakening, perhaps shocking, and out-of-mind experience? When did it occur?

2. Would I like to spend more time in this realm today? Is there anything scary or threatening about it?

3. Whom do I know, personally or from afar, who exemplifies an enlightened being? What do I think their life is like?

4. What does my rationale mind think about enlightenment? If I imagine myself as fully enlightened, do any inner judgments, fears, or criticisms arise?

5. What is my vision of my life at its highest potential? My ultimate vision -- as good as it gets.

Ask

"One who asks a question is a fool for five minutes;
one who does not ask a question remains a fool
forever."
--Chinese proverb

What questions do you ask yourself each day? *Those* questions are perhaps the most important ones of tall because the questions you ask determine your success and happiness in life. That is, it's not your IQ, EQ, Rolodex, or even your life experience that determines your success and happiness in work, relationships, money, and life. Instead, the questions you ask shape what happens to you and for you. Ask yourself great questions. Lead a great life. Ask yourself poor questions… you get the idea.

Need proof? Choose any great person, living or past, and based upon their actions, you should be able to infer the important life questions he or she consciously asked. For example, based on their life actions, we can infer the questions of Einstein, Buddha, and Martin Luther King Jr. quite easily.

Einstein's life question: "What is the mind of God?"

The Buddha: "What is the secret to a lifetime of happiness?"

Martin Luther King Jr.: "What is the best path for racial reconciliation?"

Over a lifetime of sincere, dedicated self-inquiry, each realized a valuable inner discovery: $E=mc^2$, The Middle Way, and non-violent protest, respectively. So what is your life's question? It's good to know because the questions you consistently ask determine your motives and direction in life. Here's why:

Questions, conscious or not, focus your attention on an outcome. There's a really simple rule in life: you get more of whatever you focus your CONSISTENT ATTENTION on. The questions you ask frame your life's perspective, choices, and actions. Asking yourself sincere and dedicated questions opens up space within for new answers and insights to emerge. Asking trains your inner knowingness to become even more knowing and powerful. You attract to yourself the inner answers as well as the external people, resources, and events to bring you that which you seek. There's not a single question that won't ultimately fall to sincere and dedicated seeking.

Asking yourself questions develops that all-knowing place within you to respond as easily as if you called a friend on the phone. But *this* call is made to a place within you that already has all the answers. Sooner or later, you'll get your insight. You then begin to ask new questions, get answers, and ask even greater ones. By your own volition, you move yourself up the evolutionary spiral one question at a time. A life can be traced back to its questions.

Consequently, if you're on the path to enlightenment, then your life must also be driven by a really great and very conscious question. Questions such as "How can I be more loving and accepting?" "How can I best express my true calling?" "How can I experience lasting freedom?" "How can I experience more bliss?" "How may I best serve?"

For most of us however, our lives are driven by hidden, subconscious questions that make our lives feel less than blissful. Here are some common refrains: "How can I feel worthy?" "How can I keep control?" "How can I avoid being hurt?" "How can I win the acceptance of others?"

It's our hidden answers to these programmatic, dark, secret questions that form our subconscious conditioning and develop our ego and personalities. *Why?* Why do you do what you do? The answer to "why" reveals your life's question.

Before I woke up, my life's question was "How can I feel 'good enough?'" Everything I've done in life, I can trace to an unmet need to feel more worthy, more accepted, more safe or "good enough." This feeling of not being good enough ran my life. I can trace its origins back to my childhood--so far back, in fact, that I go to the womb.

One scene that jumps to mind is of me as a little boy of six sitting on the school bus for my first day of school. I am really nervous. My head is down. I'm avoiding eye contact with the other kids. I feel a sense of anxiety running throughout my chest. I just don't want to be seen. Finally, as we're approaching the school, I'm thinking, "Good, no one noticed me." And then it hits.

An older kid, say 7 or 8, calls out, "Hey you, yeah you," pointing at me. "What's wrong with your eye? You got a lazy eye or something?"

My worst fear is materializing. I am blushing with shame. "Na-u-o-h," I stammered. "It'sth not lazthy. It just doesthn't work right."

The kid shouts to the rest of the bus, "Ha ha that guy has a lazy eye and a lisp!" "Hey man, look at that kid's eye." "What a loser."

No big deal. One young kid teasing another. Happens all the time. But it is a big deal in my mind. What some 8-year-old says to me on the bus more deeply reinforces a pattern of "I'm not good enough" into my subconscious. I repeatedly, unconsciously and consciously, tell myself that I'm not good enough. My deepest unstated fear is that I've been abandoned to the scrap heap of the world. Who would give a bum eye, a lisp, and these painful feelings to a kid? I *must* not be good enough. On and on the conditioning goes. One small life event compounding on another.

Later in life, even when I thought I had a pretty good handle on the depth and nuances of this unconscious conditioning, new formations of it continued to emerge in my life. This stuff goes very deep and can even get kind of weird.

I remember one instance during my transition to becoming more self-aware that exemplifies how deep and far back these unconscious patterns can go. At the time, I was sincerely asking myself, "Why do I feel the way I do? What contributes to this feeling of 'not good enough' that runs my life?"

One afternoon, my wife Shanna and I were in our marriage counselor's office, exploring how different unconscious patterns play out in our relationship. As the counselor is speaking to me, over her shoulder a very real looking "movie clip" suddenly appears and begins to play, hovering in midair.

'Ok, this is weird,' I say to myself. 'There's a movie playing out of thin air.' I watch, enthralled, and am pretty sure that I've gone crazy. The clip takes place on the water at the foot of a large castle on a bluff. The castle is burning. There's the sound of battle everywhere. Men are shouting and searching for something. On the water, there's a small boat surrounded by reeds. In the boat is a queen, her guards, and a small baby wrapped in cloth.

I instantly get that I'm the little baby in the clip. The queen, who is enchantingly beautiful with beguiling eyes, is looking down at me with both love and sadness. I can tell instantly that she's my mother. She is crying. The men in the boat tell her that she's in danger and we must leave now. She hugs me one last time, says "I love you," places me in a small basket of reeds and sets me adrift in the water.

I feel totally and completely abandoned. What's going to happen to me? What have I done wrong that my mother would give me up unprotected? What's a helpless baby going to do? The clip disappears. The sound of the room comes back into my awareness.

I think to myself, 'Oh, great, I've got a Moses complex!' I interrupt the counselor and tell her what I just witnessed. "Have I gone crazy?" I ask.

She doesn't laugh at me. She points out how the subconscious can often speak to us in metaphor so that we can understand. She feels that it represents a very early state of feeling abandoned by my mother.

"Whew," I said. "Ok that makes sense to me, but its still pretty fricking weird."

I later shared with my mom this vision and asked her about it. "Mom, did you ever feel like abandoning me early in life?" She confirmed that she always loved me and never wanted to give me up.

However, as I described the vision, she said the castle actually sounded like a place she stayed at in Portugal when she was pregnant with me. She showed me a picture of the place--it actually was a castle on a bluff--and my jaw dropped. It was the exact image from my vision. I had never seen it before then. She also shared with me how she and my father had a terrible fight there one night. According to her (I'm sure my dad has a different version) he felt unattracted to her because she was getting "fat" during the pregnancy. This of course was his unconscious conditioning at play. My mother felt terrible. Unloved, unprotected, and attacked. They had a loud argument in the room that night. She was crying. I'm sure a part of her felt like giving me up and being thin again.

'Ah ha!' I think. 'There's my original feeling of abandonment, of not being good enough.' It goes all the way back to the womb. I don't know, perhaps it goes back even further.

"How can I feel 'good enough?'" is not a question that's going to take anyone very far in life. Sure, it can lead to lots of outward achievement. In fact, this or a similar question unconsciously drives many of the most outwardly successful people I know. They don't feel good enough, worthy enough, or safe enough on the inside, which is why they attempt to compensate by being more successful, domineering, controlling, winning, etc., on the outside. These are hollow victories that don't satiate our unmet inner needs. Trying to feel worthy enough or good enough from the outside in is like going to a banquet and leaving hungry. It's an outward success driven from a place of fear. It's a fear that can't ever be beaten this way.

In essence, during my entire life, I was subconsciously saying, 'I don't feel good enough on the inside. How can I feel good enough? Here I'll try this… Nope. Maybe try this… Nope not that either. Shit. What should I do now?'

It's the crises in life that cause us to look within. Crises challenge us to identify the real answers to that which we are seeking. Through a trial by fire, they inspire us to ask new and better conscious questions that take us to new heights. Thank God for problems and crises because otherwise, we'd all still be sea slugs.

As I reached my turning point by crises, I began to ask a new question of myself. Instead of an unconscious "How can I feel good enough?" driving my life I began to ask myself a more conscious "Can I realize my true Self more fully?" and feel safe, secure, and accepted on the inside regardless of what's happening on the outside. My attention began to shift from an outside-in perspective to an inside-out perspective. I didn't know it then but I was really on to something.

At first my answer to this question was something like this: "Sure, I bet I can pick up a few tips and techniques to live my life better. I'm sure it will be time well spent." But one good question begets another that reveals new and better answers leading to even better questions. As my journey got into full swing, variations on the question began to emerge.

"What does it mean, really, to be more self-realized?"

"What's the best path to get there? Can *I* get there?"

"What would I have to give up to get there?"

"Do I even want to get there? Why, or why not?"

Amazing things start to happen when you ask yourself more conscious questions. Answers reveal themselves. People show up in your life. Ideas form. Books jump into your hands. Synchronicities unfold. A whole series of unimaginable events is unleashed. But it all starts with the questions.

This notion that it all begins with the question really struck home for me one afternoon. I was having lunch at an Indian restaurant with one of my mentors and a colleague. We ordered and started our table talk. Since each of us had done our fair share of personal transformation work, the conversation naturally went towards different stories and personal experiences. We began discussing various meditation and other techniques for self-realization.

What was better, this meditation technique or that one? Was it the path through the heart or to transcend the mind? What was this teacher like? What works for you? What doesn't? That kind of thing. I knew this conversation really well. At that point, I was still in search of the perfect and superior technique to "get there" quickly. I felt as if I could just find "it" then I would transform all of my fears, doubts, and pain. But what was "it?" I looked high and I looked low. I tried many, many different things. As I sat there at the table, I had another epiphany.

"You know what," I said, "every personal transformation technique and practice is a good one. It all depends on what you need at the time. Personally, I can look back over the past year and clearly see that I've made monumental leaps in my self-awareness. I've gone farther and faster than I could ever have imagined. But I don't think it's from any particular practice or technique.

"Instead, the driving reasons are the questions I'm asking myself each day. Questions like, 'How can I realize more fully today?' or 'How can I experience more joy and bliss in my life?' 'How can I serve today?' Sure, the commitment and practices are important, but it's the questions that I'm reflecting on daily that really bring home the goods. The practices, techniques and answers I attract all support the originating question." My friends enthusiastically agreed and we moved on to other conversational topics before saying our goodbyes.

To understand why the questions you ask power your transformation, it's helpful to grasp something very important. There's one infinite power in the Universe. God, Source, Spirit, Reality, Divine Intelligence, Love. Call it what you will. Because there's only one power, you too are this power. You are an undifferentiated aspect of this same elemental stuff. This essence of you is you. You, your essence, is called to reveal itself more fully in your life. You are called to remember who and what you are.

The process of self-realization is to uncover and transform all the self-limiting and unconscious perceptions we collect through our lives that prevent us from realizing our true essence. By asking sincere questions, you start the journey towards higher and higher states of consciousness. There's a force at work here that is beyond description. By sincerely asking for more self-awareness, love, light, and truth, you access your essence, intuition, creativity, and knowingness to reveal more truth in your life.

Experts everywhere surround us. Gurus, teachers, doctors, lawyers, parents, elders, authors, speakers, and authorities of all kinds have plenty to say. "Do this, don't do that." "Eat this, don't eat that." "Follow this path, it worked for me." There's nothing wrong with this. Look, I'm doing it too. But experts can only claim expertise on their own personal truth.

In essence, each is saying, "Mr. Jones, here's what worked for me. If you do what I did, then you should get the same benefits. Don't you want to be rich, successful, beautiful, and/or enlightened like me? Just follow this path, eat this diet, take this pill, or practice this technique and you will. Guaranteed."

Is it true? Maybe. But not necessarily. Your path is unique. You life conditions are unique. You have a unique set of needs. Each "expert" is pitching his or her particular worldview. Their own technique, belief, or practice to help you get where they think you need to go. But when you start to ask yourself more conscious questions, this all changes. You stop looking outside yourself for answers. You trust yourself. You look within. You may still try and test different techniques from an array of expert resources but you do so from an inner guide, not an outer one. This is your power.

Much has been written and taught over the last century on the power of positive thinking and belief to powerfully change lives. As the American psychologist and philosopher William James (1842-1910) so aptly put it, "The greatest discovery of my generation is that a human being can alter his life by altering his attitudes of mind." The ability to ask questions and realize answers is part of that power.

Questions and affirmations are slightly different but complimentary to one another. An affirmation is a positive, powerful statement. "I am happy." "I am complete." "I am compassionate, loving, and serving." It is affirmation--also called intention--that can change your attitudes of mind. These positive, as-if statements absolutely work to help transform your world from the inside out. The key to a successful intention is repletion, belief, and embodying a positive, as if feeling that what you're affirming is already realized.

But you can only affirm what you already know to be true. An affirmation can only reinforce what you've already experienced in life. It can only take you as high as you've already been. Consider it a sort of glass ceiling to your evolution. Affirmations are very powerful, transforming, and necessary. A question on the other hand, opens you to new possibilities. It expands beyond the glass ceiling. It allows new heights and previously unrevealed realms to appear. It's never-ending and expanding. A question leads the way.

As you discover new inner answers from your self-directed questions you can use affirmations to reinforce your newfound discoveries. Consider the reciprocity of questions and affirmations. Ask yourself a new more conscious and uplifting question. Allow the answer to unfold in your life. They will come in unexpected and miraculous ways. You're training your inner self to take on more responsibility and to provide more guidance in your life. A good question takes you up a rung on the spiral of life. A good affirmation reinforces your awareness and helps keep you there.

Here's an example. When I began to ask myself, "Can I realize fully?" new experiences began to appear in my life, experiences that opened and deepened my mind to previously unknown possibilities.

One evening I was strolling down the beach just admiring the sunset. Without any forewarning or conscious intention on my part--whoooosssh--a wave of indescribable bliss washed over me. Without choice I fell to a knee and caught myself from toppling over. In an instant of renewed clarity, I felt myself as one with everything else in creation. My conscious recognition of myself expanded out into infinity. Tears of joy streamed down my cheeks. What just a moment ago was routine -- the seagulls, the sand, the sound of the waves, and the other beach walkers--now was exquisite. I could feel the essence behind the forms. Every grain of sand, rock, sea gull, cloud, and person, all of it, was radiating light, vividness, texture, and a feeling of unimaginable love. Then just as suddenly--whoooosssh--it was gone and only an astonishingly pleasant memory remained.

I was struck with the notion that the Universe just answered my question. "Oh, you want to realize more? Fantastic! Allow me to share with you a little bit more about what it's like and whet your appetite for more."

Peak experiences like this one give insight into the road ahead. They provide an advanced look and bring richer meaning to the words we use. Before experiences like these, I had no real concept of what "bliss" or "oneness" really meant. I thought I did but I only knew enough as my prior experience had shown me. I could only know them as I had known them. It didn't do me much good to affirm, "I am joyful" because my concept of joy was so limited.

But as I asked myself new and expanding questions, I experienced deeper states of living. My horizons opened. My experience deepened. Words like joy and bliss took on new meanings and context. I could then more readily affirm, "I experience joy and bliss all the time." "I am joyful. I am blissful." "Joy is my constant companion." because I had the previous experience to back the affirmations up. The questions lead and the affirmations follow.

So how do you ask yourself a question? That's another great question! Here are some suggestions. When you frame and ask yourself a question, do it with a sincere sense of wonderment. You're not looking for answers you think should be right. Allow yourself to open to new possibilities.

"I wonder…" is a great way to begin a question. After you ask, wait. Just wait for a response. It might come in an instant or it might take months to unfold. The very act of asking the question begins to unfold the process of discovery. Let your desire to know go. Just let it go. You're not looking for rapid answers or forced ones. Self-imposed time pressure will kill your response. Maintain a state of expectancy that you'll receive your answer at the perfect time.

It will come in unexpected ways. It might be a feeling, an experience, an intuitive hunch, a phone call, a new relationship, or a sign or signal from the Universe as if it's saying, "Look, I've got your answer over here."

Asking yourself questions trains your inner guru--that place inside of you that already knows all the answers--to respond more freely, readily, and clearly. As you get your answer, you begin to ask new questions, get answers, and ask even greater ones. All the while reinforcing your progress with practices that we will explore further in this book. You are moving yourself up the evolutionary ladder.

The journey towards self-realization--towards greater joy, bliss, prosperity, safety, and happiness--begins by asking yourself more conscious questions and trusting the responses you receive. This self-trust and self-dialogue nourishes your inner guru who will guide you on the path. So what questions are you asking of your life?

Five questions to ponder regarding your life's questions…

1. Can I realize myself fully in this lifetime? Do I even want to? Why or why not?

2. Am I ready for enlightenment? Why or why not?

3. What question, or questions, do I choose for myself that will lead my life in the direction I want to go?

4. I wonder what unconscious questions, doubts, fears, and negative beliefs may be contributing to my current condition?

5. *Why* do I do what I do? *Why* am I the way I am?

Commit

"...The moment one definitely commits oneself, then Providence moves too."

--Goethe

A few persons in every generation do seem to be born with expanded awareness. These "lucky" few come into life with a deep sense of knowingness about who they are and what they're called to do from very early in life.

I always felt envious of people like this. For most of my life, I had no idea who I was or what I was deeply called to do. It's taken me a third of my life to figure it out and I'm still learning. I've also read stories and met a few people who, without any effort or trying, one day just "woke up." It's as if they're going about their business, they've never really thought about enlightenment, God, or their role in the Universe, and then out of the blue, like a bolt of lightning.... Blam! They're instantly transformed. Their life and awareness from that day forward is completely changed. They recognize their Authentic Self, understand their Universal connection with all things, and experience true power, grace, bliss, and love. Amazing.

Ultimately, exponential leaps in your own self-realization will also happen "out of the blue," but there's much you can do to accelerate the entire process as well as experience tremendous benefits along the way. It makes no sense to cower through life afraid, anxious, or depressed, or to wait around apathetically for life to change in your favor.

There's a fascinating and amazing journey available right at your fingertips. It's got all of the elements of a great adventure story. There is you the hero or heroine. It includes great battles, love affairs, joys, triumphs, and life and death struggles of epic proportions. It's not a journey for the faint of heart. It's the warrior's path. It's not easy. But it is noble and worthy. Once you've begun to ask yourself an inner question such as "Can I realize fully?" you're on the path to accelerated transformation. The next step is to commit. Commit to realize your highest potential in this lifetime.

We have many options and life experiences before us so why commit to self-realization? At the end of the day, do it for no other reason than it feels good. Enlightenment is in reality a refined form of selfishness. It's selfish with a capital S. It feels *really* good to be enlightened. It's safe, secure, blissful, expansive, powerful, transcendent, and most importantly, lasting. No matter what storm is raging, you stand safe, secure, and happy within your center. Moreover, from an enlightened perspective, your definition of Self expands.

Instead of experiencing yourself as a skin-encapsulated ego concerned with me, my, and mine all day long, you view your Self as an expression of the divine inherent and one with everyone and everything else. From this vantage point, you are naturally giving, prosperous, contributing, serving, joyful, and happy all the time. Your very presence makes a powerful shift on your surrounding environment. You are able to accelerate the positive change you desire for yourself and others. You are more creative, loving, compassionate, and prosperous. Knowingness, expansiveness, power, and peace radiate from within. Productivity becomes effortless and flowing. You become fearless and deeply connected to your source. Who doesn't want more of that?

Actually, most of us don't want that. Not yet anyway. We're scared of it. We're scared of what we might have to give up to get it. We're scared of what others will think. We're scared of opening up our internal Pandora's box and letting loose what's there. To even peek at our innermost self takes courage. There are dark and scary places down there. It seems safer to keep them buried deep. What good could it possibly do to let them escape outward for the entire world to see? We're petrified to allow our inner self to unfold. We're scared of letting down our walls and false barriers of separation. We're apprehensive of letting our hardened armor crumble.

Of course we are! C'mon, who in their right mind would want to stand naked, frail, and powerless against the terrible pain of self-judgment, shame, and loathing? Who could possibly allow themselves to be open, vulnerable, and unprotected against the unimaginable ferocity of the Universe? Who in their right mind would consciously allow themselves to deeply *feel* the pain of the world and to admit to their own frailties, grief, and terror? Very, very few. It takes tremendous courage to go within. Massive cojones are required to be brave enough to truly open your heart, accept what is, and deeply feel your own vulnerable, tender, and frail humanity. As Henry David Thoreau so aptly put it, "It is easier to sail many thousands of miles through cold and storm and cannibals, in a government ship, with 500 men and boys to assist one, than it is to explore the private sea, the Atlantic and Pacific Ocean of one's being alone."

After you wake up, your entire life is an expression of love. Love of yourself, love of others, love of God. Love of the richness of experience in life. You may still do the same things you did before, but your vantage point has shifted. You've transcended your old conditioning. You see reality for what it is. Ultimately, we will all reach the point where we realize that our internal evolution is the only true path. The only real path for lasting peace and true happiness is the inward journey. We acknowledge that true success can't come at the expense of our inner growth but from the expression of it.

At the start of my transformation, I still hadn't made my commitment. I was just looking for an edge to get ahead in life. I didn't actually believe I could attain a high level of self-realization. In fact, I wasn't even sure I really wanted it. I was just seeking answers to the new questions I was asking. Things were showing up in my life. I was experiencing subtle shifts in awareness and feeling. I was doing diligent practice of meditation and self-reflection. My progress towards greater self-awareness and inner peace was noticeable but not profound. It was all very good but I seemed kind of stuck. I wanted more and I just wasn't going as far and as fast as I wanted. Everything shifted the day my commitment level changed.

There's an old saying that "a teacher learns twice" and it's true. If you really want to be an expert at something, become a teacher of it. Since I wanted more self-awareness, I decided that learning to teach meditation would be a great thing to help my own evolution. Deepak Chopra is one of my teachers and so I signed up to become a meditation instructor with the Chopra Institute in Carlsbad, Calif. There I was sitting in class learning about higher states of consciousness. The instructor was conducting an overview, according to the Vedic tradition, about how a person evolves.

According to this rich and ancient tradition, a person begins life in the base levels of consciousness of everyday living: waking, sleeping, and dreaming. At this level, it feels like you are your mind. The one who is doing the actions and the one who is thinking the actions are perceived as the same. You are deeply involved in your own experience and can often times feel overrun by it and this creates suffering.

Man, did I know that realm really well. But as a person begins to awaken they witness their own life as if they're watching a play. It's as though you're performing the actions of your life but at the same time, watching it all unfold as a detached observer. Further on, you begin to see and feel God in everything all around you. You become aware of reality at a much more subtle level. You recognize God in trees, flowers, everywhere all the time. And at the highest levels, your experience is that of being one with everything else. You still maintain a sense of individuality but realize at the ultimate level, there is no separation; "I am the Universe" and at this level desires are perfectly aligned and spontaneously fulfilled.

I'm sitting in the classroom listening to this lecture and it all sounds well and good but very far from possible for me. I mean, come on! This is real life we're talking about. I've got a business to run. Things I want to accomplish first before I go off on this big spiritual kick. I raised my hand and in effect told this to the instructor.

Being sort of curmudgeon, the instructor responded, "Well, maybe you won't experience enlightenment. That's OK. Many people *are* experiencing it now and the numbers are increasing. When one person experiences enlightenment, the vibratory level is raised for all of us. Just by being alive in this time in history, you might experience it anyway."

I sat and stewed on what the instructor said. Honestly, my ego got really charged up! What do you mean I won't experience it? Who are you to say? I'm no slacker! I'm not going to ride on someone else's coat tails and let them get all the credit.

My attitude then reminds me of the old joke about the successful businessman who dropped out to join the monastery. After a few years, he called his mom and told her, "Hi Mom, I'm doing great. I'm now second in command after the Bishop and I have 15 monks reporting to me. In a few more years, I should be running the whole thing."

We all rely on the ego to get us started on the path. We'll discuss later how we observe the ego and surrender to something infinitely more powerful.

I reflected on higher states for several days and nights. I began to ask myself new questions, "Who, or what, is God really?" "Is he, she, or it someone I can really trust?" "Do I even want to be closer to God?" "Do I want to live in joy and bliss, even if it is possible?" My answers were very conflicted and I sought to reconcile them.

As a boy, I was raised in the Methodist tradition. My family ancestry is a long line of farmers and preachers. In fact, I grew up on the Methodist Lakeside Assembly grounds on Lake Minnetonka, Minn. Every Sunday in the summer, the neighborhood would gather at the boathouse for Sunday service from a guest minister. In the winter, we'd go to a formal church across the bay. Even though my parents weren't too rigid about religion, the idea had been instilled in me that God is "up there" and we are "down here." Was there a hell? My parents told me there wasn't but it was a running bet among the neighborhood kids there was.

In my teenage years, I dropped out of church all together. It smelled of hypocrisy. The theology didn't make rational sense. Church had little bearing on my life. My parents got divorced. There was a lot of suffering in my life. I could see a lot of it in the world too. If there was a God, how could he do such things?

I didn't give too much thought to it though. I just knew it wasn't right for me any longer. My interests were sports, girls, and beer. I think the only prayer I uttered during high school was one I led before the Minnesota State Football playoffs in front of the team.

"Take a knee for prayer and repeat after me," I said. Everyone on the team looked at each other as if to ask, "What? Lex is going to lead us in prayer? This should be interesting." But they did kneel and repeated together as I intoned, "Yea though I walk through the valley of the shadow of death, I will fear no evil, for I am the biggest, meanest, baddest motherfucker in the valley. Let's go guys!"

And my greatest philosophical foray back then was probably using St. Thomas Aquinas ontological argument to try to loosen the faith of a Catholic girlfriend. This combined with a penchant for fighting, carousing, and poor study habits all helped form me into quite the piece of work. But hey, if I can awaken, *anyone* can.

In college, I began to think more sincerely about God and the nature of the Universe. Was there a God? My answer then was no. I dabbled in atheism and existentialism. In my sophomore year I wrote a paper on my newfound existential views for an English literature class. I remember very vividly the professor calling me to his desk on the day the papers were returned to us.

'Oh no,' I thought, 'I really screwed up the paper.' The paper was not easy for me to write, but it was also a lot of fun. It felt liberating. I wrote some things that were blasphemous to my old Methodist upbringing. "There is no God." "Life is what you make of it." "There is no good and no evil." "I am responsible for my own happiness." Thus spoke Zarathustra. That kind of rap. My child brain (that 4-year-old in us that never really leaves) was telling me that I was going to be struck down by lightning just for writing this stuff down. But my adult brain was on fire, 'Fuck yes!' I thought, 'enough of this BS mind control religion crap. I am free!'

I was shocked because instead of being critiqued, my professor had tears in his eyes as he told me that this was one of the best papers he had ever read by a student. He confided in me that independent thinking like this was why he became a teacher in the first place. He shook my hand and told me how I brought a sense of meaning to his career. A+. Wow. Not what I was expecting. I felt slightly embarrassed and returned to my seat. But his encouragement unleashed a wave of confidence and enthusiasm in me to explore more of life's deeper questions.

My existentialist bent didn't last very long. Living in a Universe without an orchestrating intelligence doesn't hold up to much rational scrutiny. It's also very lonely.

I began to dabble in different eastern philosophies. The eastern idea of God as the one Causal and Real source of the

Universe resonated deeply with me. It aligned with quantum physics and modern science. It bypassed the hypocrisy of the religion I was raised in. It provided some answers to much of what I was seeking.

I shed my atheist cloth and began to define myself as "spiritual but not religious" and that was about as far as I took it for a time. My interests had grown from beer, girls, and sports to entrepreneurship, success, and money. I'm sure the conscious or unconscious questions I was asking of myself back then probably sounded something like, "How can I start a successful business?" "How can I be rich, attractive, and powerful?" "Who will love me?"

It was soon after college that I began to dive more and more into personal transformation works. My motivation wasn't spiritual. It was commercial. I started my first business and it failed. Intuitively I felt that I wasn't ready for success yet on the inside and so I began a quest for answers. I found some really great and transformative stuff in various seminars, workshops and books. I was beginning to identify and release some of the unconscious conditioning that no longer served me.

This coincided with the launch of my next business venture. With newfound inner awareness this business did grow to become quite successful, grossing hundreds of millions annually. In turn, it revealed the limitations of goal setting, positive thinking, and hard work alone as a means to achieve and manage success. My marriage suffered. My health suffered. My self suffered. Ultimately, this implosion led me to this very meditation class where I found myself scoffing at the notion of higher states of consciousness.

As I reviewed my past, I admitted to myself that yes, in a perfect world I did want higher states of consciousness. My caustic dismissal of higher states was really a cover up for deeper feelings of unworthiness and fear I carried. I simply didn't feel worthy of higher states. I didn't think it was possible for me. I also began to recognize how deeply terrified I was of God.

The old childhood image of God as a capricious entity that ruled men's lives from afar was still buried very deep in my psyche. Even though I could rationalize God as the single source of all that is, I viewed God unconsciously as something to be deathly afraid of. If I wasn't perfect, if I didn't do it exactly right, if I let up for even a second, the Universe would come sweeping in and take it all away. My entire life was built on a futile fear-based effort to escape God's wrath.

To a child's mind, mother is God, the entire Universe, and the source of Life. Even though I wasn't abandoned, I *felt* that way from very early in life. Abandonment to a child feels like death. Our ego, our sense of me and mine, is formed by our early and ongoing experiences, memories, and desires. As human beings, we get so caught up in this sense of ego that we believe we are the ego. And what's the most terrifying thing imaginable to the ego? Death, shame, and abandonment are some obvious ones.

These fears were running my life. I was driven by a fear of letting up, fear of letting go, fear of being seen, and fear of not being seen. I didn't want joy. I didn't want freedom. Joy was terrifying. Freedom was a nightmare. If I had those things, I would be totally unprotected. I would be staked out on my back, vulnerable and naked for the vultures to devour. My inherent unworthiness would reveal itself to me and to the world. How terrifying! My unconscious defense mechanism was to set my goals, work hard, and do my best in a frenetic pace. See, God? See, everybody? Look how good I am? Look how successful I am? Can't you see how hard I'm trying? Can't you see how worthy and good I really am?

Another fear I held was of transforming myself so much that everything I thought was important no longer would be. What if it turns out that at higher states I'm no longer interested in running a business? What if money and prestige no longer matter to me? What if I lose everything I've worked so hard for? What will people think of me? Won't they laugh and ridicule at this kind of freaky, lovey, head-in-the-cloudsey Lex?

These were very real fears. Many of their vestiges still linger. We all play out these unconscious stories and conditioning in our lives. The process of self-realization is to uncover the self-limiting conscious and unconscious fears we carry and transform them with love. Through love, we become more real. Ultimately, we stand completely one with God. One with all. We bask in bliss, prosperity, power, and authenticity. Commitment is the extent of how far you're willing to go. How much and how fast are you willing to release anything that's hiding your true essence from shining forth?

I took a look at my conflicting feelings about God, enlightenment, and who I really wanted to become. Intellectually, I knew that my beliefs about a capricious God "out there," abandonment, and unworthiness were false. They didn't hold up under scrutiny. They didn't serve me, even if they seemed to continue to hold themselves in deep, dark places of my psyche. I reconciled that if I actually could live in higher states of consciousness, then whatever happened must be for my highest good. After all, if I really was going to run a large and successful business and balance my family and the rest of my life, couldn't I do it better from a higher state of consciousness? If my purpose wasn't what I thought it was, wouldn't it be better to find out sooner rather than later?

And wouldn't it be nice too, once and for all, to drop these painful feelings of fear, abandonment, and unworthiness that seemed to unconsciously run my life and cause all kinds of grief? Wouldn't it be awesome to stand clean, clear, and authentic with myself in the world?

I began to ask, "Why not me? Why isn't it possible for me to experience higher states in this life time?" There wasn't any good rational reason I could come up with. In fact, rationally, I concluded that God wants all of us to remember our enlightenment right now. To wake up! God is the One source, the One presence. That means we're all a reflection of that Source. Doesn't the Source want the most efficient and effective mirror possible? Isn't that the most joyful, productive, excellent state? The nature of life is to evolve, not devolve. Why not me? Screw it; I'm going to go for it!

I allowed a tiny crack, a small sliver, a mere possibility to enter my belief system that I could reach higher states of consciousness in my lifetime. I admitted to myself that I did want to experience higher states if they were available to me. I opened to the possibility of real transformation.

In a moment of inspiration, I made a commitment to myself to realize the full expression of me in this lifetime. That this would be my highest goal. Everything else would be a distant second.

With this shift in commitment, almost as if by magic, my transformation began to radically accelerate ever faster. Peak experiences of indescribable bliss became more and more frequent and longer lasting. My awareness expanded to new and previously unknown levels. Lots and lots of really wonderful things took hold within me including greater peace of mind and an opening to my own authentic power.

But I'm not going to kid you; for several years after I made this commitment, the depths of despair became darker and more all encompassing too. Many trials by fire occurred. For several tumultuous years everything in my life seemed to get both worse and better at the same time. It felt like a terrifying roller coaster ride.

One week I'd feel incredible. I'd be flying and floating through life on an incredible high, carried by a sense of power, presence, and connection moving through me. This was the good stuff. But the next week… gone. I'd fall into a black depression, a feeling of utter hopelessness when that same elevating connection disappeared. Where did it go? Would it ever come back? I'd muddle along with a feeling of emptiness in my soul that nothing could quench. Eventually, sometimes days or even weeks later, it *would* come back and often more powerfully than ever before Ahhhhhhh. Restoration. Thank God.

I came to understand this emerging connection as my Authentic Self. It seemed to leave and return many times over. There was an ebb and flow of greater consciousness emerging within me. I was waking up and learning to carry new and higher frequencies of energy. Like a snake shedding its skin, I was shedding any old ideas, patterns, relationships, and ways of living that no longer served me. I can speak from experience that when you're in the flow of life, the old skin sheds off easily. But when you cling to the old skin – old ways of thinking, perceiving, and being – it's going to rip.

This grand, elevating connection with your Authentic Self is a reminder of what you're working so hard for. It disappears from your conscious awareness when you cling too tightly to old notions of self and identity. Eventually you'll be in that positive connection all the time. But this transition period between your old self and new self can be very unsettling at times.

For example, my body would often shake uncontrollably with spasms and muscle twitches. Sometimes a shudder, like an electrical shock, would shoot down my right shoulder and out through my hand. Other times my left arm would get it. On a few occasions, I'd just have to lie down on the floor for several minutes while my whole body would convulse in waves. My hands and feet would tingle intensely. It was actually never that uncomfortable but it was unsettling to not know what was going on, when it would strike, and when it would end. I'm sure I freaked a few people out lying on the floor at yoga class flapping my arms like a giant crazed chicken.

Startling new forms of energy would often appear out of nowhere too. I remember a time when I was suffering from a lingering stomach ailment. It wasn't debilitating but there was a constant burning sensation in my upper abdomen. I was trying lots of things to clear it including diet changes, homeopathy, and energy healing but nothing seemed to work. This went on for several months.

Then one night I awoke sitting up in bed. There was a strange and powerful light filling the room. A wooshing, static sound, like a broken gas main mixed with white noise, filled my hearing. I looked down and the light was coming from inside my abdomen and radiating two to three feet outwards with unimaginable power. I wasn't scared. I felt peaceful but the power of this light was humbling. It had that fierce heatless heat to it and the color looked like the inside of a warp coil on Star Trek. I put my hands on my stomach and they seemed to fade into nothingness. Something inside me told me everything was all right. There was nothing to be scared of. I laid back down on the bed as the energy just swept over me. I eventually fell asleep again. I awoke the next morning feeling terrific and my stomach ailment was gone for good. Strange stuff.

Still at other times I'd be overtaken by waves of uncontrollable laughter. Literal gut wrenching, hold on to something solid, tears in the eyes laughter. There's only one problem: I wasn't laughing at anything. Nothing was funny. Just out of the blue, waves of laughter would come pouring out of me. It felt like being back in grade school when the teacher would threaten you to stop laughing "or else" and that only made you laugh even harder. This would go on for 5 to 15 minutes or more and then fade away.

So these types of transition experiences can be a little unsettling. But don't worry too much about them. They are only temporary and actually quite fascinating to experience. Whatever quixotic forms your transition to higher living take--feelings of bliss followed by periods of depression, muscle twitching, laughter, energy vortexes, or something else entirely--you'll eventually integrate this emerging connection with your Authentic Self more fully and these kinds of things will stop all together.

In addition to the unsettledness of the transition period, going back to your old life can also seem very surreal. What was commonplace before now has an air of strangeness to it. One surreal moment I remember vividly is when I was invited back to my old company to give a speech to a user group of several hundred people.

I had been away from the scene for two or three years. This was a company that I played a founding and crucial role in building. It was my life and passion for many years. I went to the conference and rather than feeling like I returned home, it felt like I was walking on Mars. The energy, the frenetic pace, the focus on cutting deals, making dollars, winning the game. It was like a shark pit. "I started this thing?" I asked myself incredulously. I no longer resonated with it at all.

But what did I resonate with? I wasn't sure. I had a very hard time finding my new groove in the world. I had increasing awareness but no solid footing. This was especially true with my career. I couldn't go backwards and do what I did before. But what should I do to go forward and earn a livelihood that supported our lifestyle and the emerging me? I desperately wanted to find a new way in the world. One that matched my growing awareness and desire to make a positive contribution, express my creativity, and be in service, and at the same time provide handsomely for my family.

I tried many things. First a wellness center, then a distance learning and life coaching business, then assorted consulting roles. I was able to pay the bills and maintain our standard of living but stability went out the window. My inner life was evolving so rapidly that my outer life was having a hard time keeping pace. I drove my wife nutty with a constant change in business direction. I'm pursuing this… no, not that… now I'm going to do this. It was exhausting and tiring for both of us.

But the most trying (and liberating) part of the transition process was this: All those hidden fears that ran my life unconsciously didn't dissipate after I made my commitment. Instead, they rose up in a magnified way, one after the other after the other.

For most of us, living through your fears isn't done with the excitement and flair of a Hollywood action movie. Personally, I didn't have any near death experiences. There weren't any bad guys chasing me. Instead, fears are played out in the day-to-day minutiae of every day living. If you're carrying a fear on the inside, it's going to come out on the outside in a variety of ways. When you pay close attention, you'll spot how a dark and often unstated fear plays itself out continually in your relationships, events, and life experiences.

Like an actor in a play, I got to live through all of my fears and sometimes more than once. Some days, with my connection gone, my direction unclear, and facing my biggest fears of abandonment and unworthiness, it felt like the Universe was perfectly designed to kick the living crap out of me.

Imagine that. Choosing and committing to enlightenment as your highest goal and as a reward you get to live through and experience all of your greatest fears. It doesn't sound like much of a trade. But there's a funny thing about living through your fears… you realize all fear is a paper tiger. In fact, the perceived hardship of experiencing your greatest fear actually reveals your greatest strengths. Strengths that were always there but hidden until now from your conscious awareness. Like a sword tempered by fire, you lose all fear in the heating process. And what do you gain? Freedom. Freedom from fear. Priceless.

These trials by fire are great tests of commitment. Through them all, I never lost sight of my highest goal. Transform. Evolve. Realize. Up and down the roller coaster I went trying to find the dynamic balance of an evolving being with his feet firmly planted on the ground. Ultimately, a deep and lasting connection with my Authentic Self integrated within me. Happiness, health, and prosperity are mine for the asking. To get where I am now, I'd go through all the trials again in a heartbeat.

Most importantly, I will still experience trials in life. I'm still going to suffer. I'm still going to cope with loss. This is life. But by virtue of awakening and tempering, I am blessed with a deep resiliency. I know that whatever trials emerge in the future, I will move through them with much greater ease, grace, creativity, and acceptance than was possible before.

Will you need to ride the roller coaster too? Will you have trials and tribulations? Yes! Absolutely, positively, you're going to be tested. You are going to experience pain, suffering, doubt, and terror. This is not a journey for the faint of heart. It's the warrior's path. It's the noble path. It's the most adventurous and intriguing path there is. But it's not easy. And so what? If you're life was already easy, if you weren't already experiencing pain, doubt, self-limitation, and fear, you wouldn't be reading this book. What if Odysseus just sailed out and returned home without a hitch? We'd never be reading about him, would we?

Have faith on your journey. First and foremost, there's nothing you can't handle along the way. You are powerful beyond measure. The trials and tribulations you kick up really just reveal to you how powerful you truly are. Second, there are equally powerful forces already prompting you towards enlightenment. It's almost as if you don't have a choice in the matter. But when you make your commitment, you fully unleash these forces in your life. You are going to be transformed. You will transcend all of the pain, doubt, and suffering. You will live in joy, bliss, security, and prosperity all the time. It will happen as fast as you allow it to. But to get there, you've got to go through anything and everything that's getting in the way. This is your commitment.

Imagine a mythical knight embarking on a noble quest. His orders from the King are to find the Holy Grail. He's committed to the quest. He's dedicated his life to it. He absolutely refuses to come back empty handed. He has no idea where to look or how to find it. He just holds a simple faith that he'll make his way through. On the journey he overcomes many challenges. He fights with dragons, beasts, and demons. He overcomes many mind challenging traps. He suffers. He doubts. His commitment is sorely tested.

Along the way, almost as if by magic, he also picks up many useful and beneficial things. A sword here, a good horse there, a shield from a kind stranger, an oracle to hint at the best path, an ancient book, even a talisman to give him faith and courage along the way.

Ultimately, when all seems lost, he bursts through and reaches the Grail. It is more magnificent then he could have ever imagined. He is satisfied beyond words. From his new vantage point, he reflects on his journey to arrive. He realizes that all of the trials, tests, and tribulations were necessary. They revealed his inner strength, courage, love, and wisdom. The quest for the grail, realizes the knight, was all along an inward journey. The Grail was always there, right within reach. But it was the hardships that transformed him from the inside out. They revealed the inner blocks and fears halting his way. His newfound appreciation for the trials was profound. "Thank God for my commitment,' says the Knight. "Thank God for the trials."

So what kinds of trials and tribulations can you expect on the journey towards enlightenment? It depends on what's false in your life. On this trip you only have to allow what's real to transform what is false. When everything is real, then there's nothing else to transform. Put another way, the trials and tribulations aren't real at all. They're false. Your journey is to find what's real and experience and express more of that. You only have to travel as far as the last false thing. When you find and transform the last false thing, you are authentic and never have to be false again. This is self-realization.

What is false in your life? It's really simple--and not so simple. Here's what I mean...

Everything that can be perceived in the material Universe is real but not *real* at the same time. All the physical stuff around us has a dimension in time and a dimension in space. For example, look at a building in your neighborhood. Does it have a dimension in space? Sure. It has a length, width, and a height or a size and a shape. It takes space. Does it also have a dimension in time? It does. At one point in time, there was no building on that plot. Then later it was constructed. At some point in the future it will be no more. This is true for everything in the physical Universe: your body, your house, your car, your country, and your planet, all of it. Everything that appears material resides in time-space. It has a beginning and an end, a size and a shape.

Even the more subtle aspects of the material Universe have a time-space component. Light waves, for instance, exist in time and space. A light wave has a shape. It exists in time. Even your thoughts have a time and space component. While a thought is harder to discern in space than a building or light wave, it does occupy some spatial quality. It occupies space in your mind. It also occupies space in the Universe. Your thoughts also have a time component. A thought has a beginning, middle, and end. You weren't thinking of something, you began to think about it, you stopped thinking about it. Everything that can be perceived exists in time and space.

Intellectually, we know too that all matter that exists in time and space--be it as heavy as a planet or as light as a thought-- is really energy. Einstein made if very clear: $E=mc^2$. The entire Universe is made up of highly complex, infinitely varied, intelligently orchestrated energy fields. These energy fields coalesce and form into different patterns that take shape in the material Universe.

(Stay with me. We're identifying what is false in order to reveal what is real.)

The human brain is the instrument of our perception. It works in the realm of time and space. It is designed to perceive these energy waves and form them into recognizable patterns – patterns such as butterflies, dogs, buildings, and your parents. Different brains perceive different things. Imagine a chair sitting alone in a room. A bat brain perceives an electro-magnetic frequency of the chair. A chameleon brain actually perceives two chairs. A human brain sees a chair, but even that is open to interpretation. What does it signify? What does it remind you of? What color is it? Ask any two people and you'll get two different perceptions.

You are not your brain. Your brain simply interprets energy waves through the five senses. Because energy is constantly moving it has a frequency or a rate of movement over time. Faster moving energy fields have higher frequencies. Slower moving energy fields have lower frequencies. Some frequencies we can detect with our senses. We see in light frequencies, hear in sound frequencies, smell in scent frequencies, taste in taste frequencies, feel in feeling frequencies, think in thought frequencies, and even our bodies and the physical world are made up of combinations of slower moving, lower frequencies that are solid to the touch.

Do you have a hard time imagining everything you can experience as a frequency of energy? If so, try this little experiment. Imagine that you can amp up the perception of your brain so that your human eyes, instead of perceiving the slower moving frequencies of light and matter, are now capable of perception like a high-powered microscope.

Now look at your hand. What do you see? You see that your hand isn't really a hand at all. It's a dynamic energy field, moving and oscillating at tremendous speed generating a pattern or frequency. Next, go back to your normal vision and allow your perception to go within. Bring your attention to the palm of your hand. Feel the blood course through your fingers and palm. Blood is a collection of molecules and corpuscles that are made up of atoms that are made up of very fine energetic frequencies called electrons, protons, and neutrons. Energy.

Ready for Enlightenment?

Bring your two palms close together without touching. You'll feel a different kind of frequency between and perhaps even surrounding your hands. Do you feel it? Energy. Now bring your attention to your heart beating in your chest. Just feel its rhythm that is conducted by an electrical frequency. Energy.

Recall a time in your life when you felt really teed-off. When you were feeling incredible anger, rage, or resentment. Do you have a time in mind? If so, then you'll notice the frequency shift in your heart. It probably feels tighter and more constricted than just a moment ago. Now take a few deep breaths and let these feelings go.

Next, think of a time when you felt sincere joy, gratitude, and appreciation for someone or something in your life. Recall the event and notice the positive feelings, the higher moving frequencies entering your heart. Your heart, which in essence is just a big frequency pump, will likely feel lighter and more expansive. The material Universe is energy frequencies that exist in time and space, including your body, emotions, and thoughts.

Other frequencies, the vast majority, are beyond our senses altogether. We can't discern radio frequencies with our five senses but nevertheless they are there. We can't discern x-rays, ultra-violet rays, and gamma rays either but science tells us they are there. On the other hand, science can't yet measure the frequency of love. Does this mean love doesn't exist? Of course not. You don't need a scientist to tell you love exists. It is self-evident. Perhaps one day, science will be able to measure the frequency of love just as it has been able to discover radio, electricity, and gravitational waves. If we do, it doesn't mean love has been discovered. We've simply developed our capabilities to detect what has always been there.

So all this stuff that we can perceive--stuff with our senses, with scientific equipment, from our experience--it all exists as energy in time and space. What does this mean? It means that none of it is *real*. All of it is temporary. It exists and then it doesn't. How can something that is temporary truly be real?

I'm not denying the existence of the material Universe. It's not simply all an illusion. It does exist. It is real. Jump off a cliff and the laws of the physical Universe are going to ensure that you hit the ground. It's just that it all exists temporarily, so that you jumping off the cliff has a beginning and end in time and space. It is transitory. Anything that is temporary and fleeting is not permanent and therefore can't be real.

Now let's go even further and see if we can identify what is real. Go back to your microscope eyes. Increase your perception even further to that of a super duper high-powered level that can see even beyond the energy fields that comprise the material Universe. What would you see then? You'd see that beyond the physical world and beyond the energy fields comprising the physical world--everything comes from One source. Intuitively and rationally this makes sense. After all, doesn't everything have to come from some place? If it didn't, it couldn't even exist. Nothing comes from nothing. Everything comes from something. A child comes from a parent. The galaxy comes from the Big Bang. What does the Big Bang come from?

Ultimately, at the finest levels, everything must come from something real, something that is beyond time and space. Correspondingly, this means that everything that exists in time and space must be an aspect of the same stuff. All is literally One. As the quote from the legendary physicist and contemporary of Einstein David Bohm put it, "Individuality is only possible if it unfolds from wholeness."

What is this stuff from which everything else comes? It's Real. It's God. It's Source. It's Divinity. It's Love. Call it what you will. Everything else is an expression, a variation in time and space, of this original real stuff.

At this ultimate real level, there is a) no time, b) no space, c) no end, d) no differentiation, and e) no experience.

> **About Language**
>
> Throughout much of the rest of this book, I'm going to use the term God to refer to what is real. If the word God is uncomfortable for you (it was for me for a long time) then please choose a more suitable word that aligns with your preference. Here are some synonyms that may better suit your personal preference:
>
> *Absolute, All That Is, Allah, Atman, Brahman, Buddha-Mind, Christ Consciousness, Creative Energy, Divine Intelligence, First Cause, Intelligence, Life, Love, Reality, Source, Spirit, Tao, The Indivisible Whole, The One Power and Presence, The Universal, Truth, Unified Field...*

If God is the single real source for everything and everything in the material Universe unfolds from this God stuff, what characteristics can we know about God? No one can really know God because God is beyond description. However, there are several things we can infer.

God is real. We can discern that God must exist beyond time and space. If God were only within time and space, then it would be fleeting and temporary and unreal. Something must be real for the temporary to exist. Everything must come from something. God is the name we give to the real. In fact, God is the only true reality. Everything else is temporary.

God is everywhere and within everything. The stuff we perceive with our senses and instruments cannot exist independently of the stuff that created it. Just as a child has characteristics of the mother and father within it, all the stuff that we perceive must also have the same real source it came from within it. This temporal Universe exists within and from a real blueprint. Therefore, within all the stuff we perceive, God also exists. God is everywhere and within everything. Reality is everywhere within the forms we perceive.

God is creative. It is the ultimate creative force in the Universe. We can see this creativity in how the Universe unfolds in increasing levels of complexity. This creative force, this will to evolve and expand, is ever present. If God were not creative, nothing would exist. There would be no originating creative impulse.

God is silent and still. Music without silence cannot be heard. A bow launches the arrow from stillness. God is the originating source and so it must also be silent and still. If it was not silent and still, nothing could be created into the realm of form.

God is intelligence, thus life is intelligence, and life is God. Nature has a divine intelligence that even a child can see. Plant a pumpkin seed and a pumpkin grows. Put your attention on your heartbeat. Feel its rhythm beating in your chest. What is beating your heart? Digesting your food? Regenerating your body? Innate intelligence is doing that. Life is doing that. And life is intelligence.

God is self-aware. God must be self-aware because it is only consciousness that can recognize itself. If God were not conscious then nothing would be conscious. There would be nothing to reflect, nothing to perceive, nothing would exist. It requires consciousness to perceive itself.

God is perfection. Imagine in this field of pure potential and creative expression that is God that any flaw existed. If a flaw did exist, the Universe would instantly implode on itself and be destroyed. There would be no intelligence; there would be no Universal laws such as gravity, quantum entanglement, electricity, time, or space because the flaw would create havoc in everything. With even a small flaw, nothing would exist and all would be chaos. God is perfect.

God is you. God is within everything and everyone. God is all that is. Therefore you are real. You are timeless, eternal, undifferentiated, whole, silent, still, creative, intelligent, self-aware, and perfect. This is the real you. What is false in your life are any artificial conscious and unconscious beliefs you hold that tell you otherwise. Beliefs and perceptions rooted in fear, separation, self-limitation, and denial are false. What is real in your life is the only real power in the Universe. Self-realization is to reside more fully in this one and only reality--the reality of Truth.

So you are already realized. Anything or anyone that communicates to you otherwise is false. The path to enlightenment is to uncover and release anything and everything that is masking reality. This is where it gets simple--and not so simple--at the same time.

It's simple because your experience of life is simply a reflection of your beliefs. Beliefs are created by perceptions. Perceptions are created by the mind. The mind perceives falsely. Therefore, change your beliefs and you change your reality.

It's not so simple because you are unconscious of the vast majority of your beliefs. You've gathered them up through life like lint on a lint brush. When you commit to your highest realization, God responds by providing situations and experiences to point out any and all false and self-limiting beliefs you carry. The greater your commitment to self-realization, the greater your power to transform, and the more transformative opportunities you will attract. When you commit to realize your highest potential, in effect you are committing to clean out any false and self-limiting gunk that stands in the way of your full self-realization.

Imagine yourself as a homing beacon sending out a powerful signal. When you consciously commit to finding and experiencing your fullest realization, you change your signal. As sure as the law of gravity, God responds.

"Oh, you want enlightenment? OK, no problem, I would love for you to experience whatever it is that you want. We are one. As you experience more, I experience more too.

But there are a few things you have blocking the full reception of my broadcast. Here, allow me to point them out to you."

We've all had the experience of consciously asking and committing to something positive in our life, and getting what appears to be the exact opposite. Guess what? You're in the process of attracting what you want. You want something. God orchestrates the Universe to deliver it. But if there's a false belief that prevents its manifestation, God's first going to point that out.

"I'd love to give you this new car you've asked for or something even better. However, you've got to give up this self-limiting poverty consciousness in order to have it. Here allow me to magnify how it's contributing to your feeling of lack and limitation. With enough pain, perhaps you'll be ready to finally give it up."

This can be confusing and discouraging because we're not often fully aware of the false or unconscious beliefs that we carry. Your commitment is tested. You doubt, rage, fight, or give up but God--the one real source within you and the entire Universe--continues to point them out until you become fully aware and clear them. Clearing them, or allowing them to release, is the *practice* of self-realization. Let's explore what it means to practice this release in the next chapter.

Five questions to ponder regarding your commitment to enlightenment…

1. What is my highest goal in life?

2. How committed am I to my enlightenment?

3. How do I demonstrate this commitment today?

4. How can I demonstrate it more fully?

5. What other commitments have I chosen that keep me from being fully self-realized?

Practice

"Why not let people differ about their answers to the great mysteries of the Universe? Let each seek one's own way to the highest, to one's own sense of supreme loyalty in life, one's ideal of life. Let each philosophy, each world-view bring forth its truth and beauty to a larger perspective, that people may grow in vision, stature and dedication."

--Algernon Black

Self-realization requires practice. Lots and lots of practice. What are you practicing? *Being real*. The process of self-realization is to peel back the layers of the proverbial onion. To uncover and transform the many layers of false, but seemingly real, mental, emotional, and physical gunk that can seem to cover up your direct experience of reality.

When we're aligned with reality we experience love, joy, bliss, and power at our core. The deeper and more pure our connection, the more perfection we experience. What gets in the way of our connection? Nothing. It's all God. Everything is *real* at the finest level. What we perceive as the good, the bad, the beautiful, and the ugly is all made from the same stuff. Everything is an expression of the same divine thing. But our perceptions, habits, and false viewpoints can clog our connection to reality and we can forget this fact. Self-realization is to remember.

Imagine a clogged drain. There's lots of gunk and goo down in the pipes that blocks fresh and enlivening water from flowing. To get the water flowing again you've got to unclog the drain. Similarly, we're also swimming and starving in gunk and goo. There's physical gunk, emotional gunk, intellectual gunk, even some soul gunk. You've got it. I've got it. We've all got some amount of gunk to clear out of our "pipes" or we wouldn't even be here. When we clear it out we realign with Source, the water of life, and experience its vital and enlivening flow. We remember who we are. We see reality for what it truly is. We experience ever-increasing fields of self-realization. It's a total blast.

There are many ways to practice being real. Entire traditions and cultures have been built around them. There's nothing I can add to the voluminous traditions from great minds and spirits on how to practice being more real. Buddhism, Christianity, Hinduism, Judaism, Gnostic Traditions, Islam, Mysticism, Naturalism, Paganism, Shinto, Sufism, Vedanta, and countless others all will take you there. Any tradition can take you there. New traditions can take you there. The secret is that you are already there.

The perennial philosophies all point to the same direction. All state that there is something real behind the veil of the senses. Enlightened living is the process of revealing what *is*. The closer you get to reality, the more superior living and the more joy, prosperity, happiness, and peace you and everyone around you experiences.

Regrettably, the perennial philosophies have all been misconstrued and manipulated over the eons. It's tiring for me to point out the countless wars, violence, terror, domination, destruction, and perversion of these great perennial truths caused by man's fear, greed, and desire to control. Fundamentalism will eventually kill itself. Pluralism and an environment of mutually respectful spiritual exploration of all traditions and paths is the way forward.

I have my personal collection of favorite traditions and practices. You have your own favorite traditions and practices. This is grand! What works well for me may not work as well for you and vice versa. Let us help one another on the path, not by comparing one practice over another, but by lovingly supporting each other on the journey. There are many doors and one destination. Everything is connected. When any soul reaches higher states of truth, we all benefit.

An open inquiry is the spirit of self-discovery that I choose to cultivate with one very important qualification; it is not *what* you practice but *how* you practice that really counts. When it comes to any practice of being more real, it's not what you do; it's how you do it.

A friend told me recently about the time he was at a personal growth conference of one type or another. The keynote speaker asked the audience, "How many of you have been to a seminar like this one in the past year?" About half the audience raised their hand.

"How many of you have read a book about this subject in the past year?" Even more people raised their hands.

"All right," he said jokingly, "stand up, turn around, and walk out."

He continued, "You're not going to learn anything new today that you haven't already heard before. You already know what to do. Your challenge is how to do it. That takes practice, persistence, and determination and that's what I'm going to focus my talk on today…"

I like this story because it rings really true for me on my own journey. During my odyssey, I became a seminar junky. I was meditating, contemplating, and trying to transform all the time. I was reading more books each week than ever before. I turned over many stones looking for the secret practice or technique that would help me transform. In a quest for more and more self-understanding, I made it my career to learn and evolve.

I learned new forms of meditation, stress management, prayer, and relationship skills. I discovered new techniques for developing creativity, self-awareness, and greater joy. I dove into new philosophies of human growth and planetary evolution. I read about quantum physics and alternative medicine. I learned about joyful money, the quiet mind, and living your purpose and passion. I invested a small fortune on multiple visits and advanced tests with leading holistic medical doctors on my health, diet, metabolism, and energy levels.

I felt a strong pull to discover more and more about the subtler aspects of life. I spent considerable time and money to become certified in various new disciplines. Some were esoteric like distance healing and energy medicine and others were more ordinary but equally interesting such as change management theory. I wasn't following any set program. I was just keenly interested to discover and grow. Here are a few examples:

I was conscious of the visceral reactions my mind-body experienced from stress. I could feel these reactions but not control them. I wanted to understand and manage those unconscious responses better so I became a biofeedback technician with the Neurotherapy and Biofeedback Certification Board based in Black Mountain North Carolina. This, in conjunction with hands on certification with energetic wellness devices such as the QXCI and BioMeridian, taught me about homeopathy, acupressure points, and how to control and relieve the negative imprints of stress on the mind-body.

I was learning about chakras, meridians, and distance healing but couldn't really fathom those things within myself. To experience them first hand, I became a Reiki practitioner with the Usui Reiki Center in Santa Barbara, Calif. After the training, all those things I was learning about made greater sense. I experienced distance healing (literally healing others at a distance) and my hands became much more sensitive to subtle energies.

I was accessing more creativity and intuition in my life but it seemed hit or miss. I came across a new concept called heart-intelligence that demonstrates how the heart strongly influences stress, creativity, and intuition. I wanted more access to that emerging heart-center and so I became a Heart Intelligence coach with the Institute of Heart Math in Boulder Creek, Calif. I benefited from increased awareness on the power of the heart as well as the ability to control and influence its rhythm to access those deeper parts of me.

I had an innate need to try to make sense of the rapid social shifts and conflict occurring on our planet. I learned about cutting edge social theory from a certification program with the Spiral Dynamics Institute based in Denton, Tex. I still greatly appreciate this data-tested framework to understand, discuss, and influence individual and collective evolution.

I wanted to understand the art and practice of meditation and learn more about the ancient Ayurvedic tradition of India so I became a meditation teacher with the Chopra Institute in Carlsbad, Calif. I learned more of the history of the Vedas and deepened my meditation and self-healing practices.

And when it came to running a business, I wanted a real-world method to orchestrate lasting organizational shifts that would help others evolve too. I was fortunate to have one of the world's leading organizational change management consultants right in my back yard, the Adizes Institute in Carpinteria, Calif., in which I also became certified to teach and practice.

There was more. It was a massive amount of seeking and learning. And I'd like to think that I'm just getting started. Life *is* learning. For those who are interested, I've included a description of many of the resources I've found helpful (so far) in the Appendix.

So for several years I was fanatical about finding the best methods for self-realization. It was all consuming. I wanted *the* solution; the suite of uber-practices that would make my enlightenment occur quickly. I was not prejudiced. If I felt something could help me on a physical, emotional, intellectual, or soul level, I'd explore and investigate. My biggest take away from my quest for answers, techniques, and solutions is this:

> There is no secret. There is no single solution. There is no best path.

As long as something helps you to experience the reality of Truth more clearly and gives respect and space to other philosophies, any personal and spiritual development practice is a good one. Depending on who you are, where you are, and what your needs are, they can all work.

About Money

When I tell people about my "career" of personal growth, I often get asked, "How did you pay for a career like that?" Or, "I'd love to do that kind of personal development trip but I don't have the money." It comes up frequently enough that I'd like to address it.

For the record, when I started this quest, I didn't have the money either. I had six months of severance and a family to support. I had no idea what I would do after that money ran out. But I just kept on keeping on and money kept appearing from sources I couldn't even have guessed at when I began. There was a constant source of supply supporting both my family and my quest. The more open I was to receive, the more I received.

With hindsight, I can see how a divine plan unfolded to support my evolution. But there were many times, especially early on, when I was deeply scared about not having enough. What if I'm fooling myself? What if I lose the house? What if I have to go back to my old corporate life?

> In reality I had nothing to fear. Money always showed up and always from unexpected sources. I never once had to reach, struggle, or stretch for it… other than the melodrama I created in my own mind.
>
> If you're called to the path, don't let a lack of money hold you back. You can always get more money. Time is the more precious commodity. When one minute is gone, it's gone. Just know that when you're ready to do what you're deeply called to do, the Universe will absolutely support you.
>
> Also, as you become more self-realized, your attraction power naturally increases as well. You gain the ability to more easily and powerfully attract all kinds of good things to you. If and when your attention is focused on wealth and true prosperity, you will soon be attracting money and resources galore.
>
> There are several great works on the subject of true prosperity and the law of attraction. I've included some of my favorites in the Appendix as well.

How do you know your practice leads you closer to reality? In essence because after some time with the practice, you feel good and the more you practice, the better you feel. You, at your Source, your Authentic Self is *real*. Everything else is an expression of that same real Source.

When you reside there, integrated and aligned within your foundation, then you feel *really* good. A deep and permanent sense of peace, awareness, wholeness, integration, love, bliss, transcendence, knowingness, happiness, and an indescribable ineffability both consume and emanate from you. It is awesome. You don't feel these things because of something; you feel them because you *are* these things. This is *reality*. You are it. Any time that you are feeling anything other than happiness and peace, it is only serving as a reminder to get back in touch with God within you. As the great Sufi poet Rumi so eloquently put it, "If you could get rid of yourself just once, the secret of secrets would open to you. The face of the unknown, hidden beyond the Universe would appear on the mirror of your perception."

As you go through life, your actions, memories, and desires generate gunk that stops the pure flow of connection with the real Source. This gunk vibrates at a lower, slower rate than your real foundation, and like a drain clog, it clogs the channel. The more gunk-collecting activities you engage in and the longer you do them, the more gunk you collect. If you spend a lifetime eating low frequency processed foods, watching low frequency violent, sensational media, or engaged in low frequency addictions such as alcohol, cigarettes, drugs, etc. then you collect a lot of gunk to clear. In this life or the next one.

A spiritual practice is anything that helps to clear out the gunk and restore the flow or reality within your being. It's actually really easy to get hits of reality. We can get them at anytime, anywhere, and while engaged in any activity. These blips and hits of Truth peak through the gunk and inspire us for more. As we continue our questions, commitment and practice, those hits and blips move out the gunk more rapidly and we experience longer, more powerful real flows of the good stuff.

Infinite opportunities for greater knowingess and expansion exist everywhere because reality is everywhere. They occur when we pierce the veil. On the journey to enlightenment, these little glimpses of something indescribable begin to get more frequent until they make up an entirely new level of existence. Meditation, for example, is such a powerful spiritual practice because it works at a very fine level. It transcends the physical body, emotions, and intellect and reaches the soul. Over time, by the regular practice of quieting down, it clears out the gunk at a physical, emotional, mental, and soul level and restores the flow of real well-being. But even the most mundane activity, when done consciously and with commitment, is an authentic practice too. A long run or a good workout not only clears out the gunk on a physical level, it provides emotional and mental benefits as well. In fact, arduous physical exercise such as running a marathon also provides feelings of transcendence that bypass the mind altogether. For many, this is a spiritual experience.

Any activity or practice, when free of dogma and control, can contribute to your greater well-being and increased awareness. Be it New Thought or Ancient Wisdom. Tai-chi or Qi-Gong. Zen Mediation or Transcendental Mediation. Hatha Yoga or a 5-mile run. Alternative medicine or traditional medicine. Hyperbaric oxygen chamber where you lie down in an oxygen tent or pranayama breathing where you learn to harness and control your own breath. Goal-setting or intention-setting. Esoteric acupuncture or Ayurvedic massage. Conscious eating or 21st century prayer. It's all good. All have their place. All to varying degrees, large or small, help you to clear out the gunk on a physical, mental, emotional, and soul level and bring you closer to the flow of reality. All can help in there own way to propel you along the path towards finer and finer levels of self-realization.

There are many, many practices for you to choose from. Countless. Find a tradition or mix and match your own. It doesn't matter. Your openness for evolution through the questions you ask and your commitment to see it happen will unfold limitless amounts of energy. The practices will take form on many levels. You practice clearing the mind, clearing your emotions, and clearing your physical body in an ever-expanding quest to feel better and better. It's that simple.

Take a meditation class and set aside time each morning and evening to go within. Find a course on better breathing and enliven your day-to-day activities. Learn to pray in a way that isn't pleading to a God-out-there but affirms and invigorates the God-within-here.

There are many practices to put in place. Find the ones that work for you and stick with them. All things come with practice. The more intense your practice, the faster you progress.

But whatever path or paths you choose, there's one thing that holds true: when you *commit* to the path of your highest self-expression, you are also committing to a lifetime of *practice*.

Imagine two men of the same age. Both have a passion and a love for the game of golf. One is an amateur. The other is a professional. Which of these two golfers has more commitment to their craft? Obviously, it's the professional. And the professional practices more too. A lot more. The higher you go in life the more you practice. Even Jesus and Buddha had to practice. Thankfully, the practice of enlightening is not dull and it's not drudgery. Most of the time, it feels really good. It's entertaining and fascinating.

The primary practice of enlightenment in any tradition, new or ancient, is to *deepen your connection to reality* and to *feel more love, compassion, and appreciation*, first for you and then for others. There are many, many paths to get there. You can transcend the mind. You can access it through the heart. You can abstain and deny what is false. Anything and everything can ultimately take you there.

Your regular practice becomes one of consciously choosing higher frequency, more life-supporting thoughts, emotions, and actions in all you do. At first, this requires great internal and external discipline. After a time, like any habit, the new choices you've developed become natural, easy, and flowing.

To always be practicing means to continually accept responsibility for your life experiences, to observe your thoughts and emotions, to reflect on them, to release those that don't serve your highest good, and to surround yourself with support from peers, like-minded community, and mentors. As you engage in these practices, you are deepening your connection to what is real and cultivating more love, compassion, and appreciation for yourself and all life.

I think a sound spiritual practice, using any method or tradition, will cover these five essential conditions: 1) self-responsibility, 2) self-observation, 3) self-reflection, 4) self-release, and 5) self-support.

Your constant practice powers your evolution. This practice is born from your life questions and commitment. The more committed you are to your own evolution, the more you practice. The more you practice, the faster and farther you go. The faster and farther you go, the more benefits you experience that in turn create greater and deeper commitment and thus greater and deeper practice. Pretty soon, in a natural and effortless way, you're flying.

Self-responsibility

Everything you experience in life is a direct reflection of your inner most beliefs. Nothing is good. Nothing is bad. It's all a reflection of you. There is no exception here, no demands from God, no luck, no misfortune, and no absolutes. To be self-responsible is to accept this and to be accountable for your life. Everything you experience, good, bad, or indifferent is created by your own deepest beliefs. No one else can harm you, help you, diminish you, or uplift you. Everything you experience in life is a mirror. The people and things you admire in life are those that you want to express more of in yourself. The people and things you abhor in life are those that you are unconsciously afraid of or fight against in yourself. There aren't any exceptions here. It's all about you.

Imagine you're walking down a city street and you see collapsed in a doorway an elderly, disheveled man. His face and hands are covered in grime. His shoes are mismatched with holes in the soles. His clothes are ragged and unkempt. He has his belongings in a shopping cart next to him. As you walk past, what inner dialogue does your belief system trigger? Is he a dirty drunk? Should he be kicked off the street? Is he a menace to society? Is he a poor soul lost at the fringes of a changing society? Is he a lazy bum? Is he a spiritual seeker renouncing material possessions? Is he a student of life doing an on-street survey? Is he a reflection of you engaged in the same journey? Regardless of who and "what" this person is, how he is reflected back to you is what's important.

If he's reflected back as a dangerous menace to society, then that's what you'll see and experience. If he's reflected back as another version of the infinite heading towards home, then how will you perceive this man? Much differently I think. To be self-responsible is to look within and accept full responsibility for the world you perceive it to be. It's all about you.

Moreover, life actually plays out according to your inner most beliefs. If you perceive a dirty, dangerous drunk in the street, that dirty dangerous drunk is going to ask you for money, puke on your shoes, and ridicule your snobbery. If you perceive the man as another aspect of your divine self, then if he responds at all, it's going to be with a shared smile, a laugh, and a deep level of heart-felt connection. Life is joy but life is also what you believe it to be.

Being self-responsible is a constant challenge. It's so easy for us to point the finger and blame someone or something else. We experience this most easily in our closest relationships. My wife and I provide a big, clear mirror back to the other. If we're having a fight, do I perceive her as being petty and belligerent or as a soul in fear needing love and unconditional support? The answer, and my level of compassion, depends on my level of self-awareness and my most inner-held beliefs about marriage, love, life, and myself. Whatever I experience, good or bad, is a reflection of my beliefs. It's never about her. It's always about me. No exceptions.

Even the most blasé interactions are a reflection of our inner state. I remember once, early in my journey, when a woman arrived late at a class I was attending. My hackles were instantly raised. There was just something about her that I couldn't tolerate. She was late, obnoxious, disorganized, and dressed like a hippy. I wanted to flee from the room and her presence. It was crazy. It was a really strong reaction.

"What did this have to say about my inner beliefs?" I asked myself.

After all, I'm not like her. I'm generally punctual, fair-minded, organized, and dressed for the part. I couldn't figure out what it was about this person. I called my wife at home to get her opinion. She wisely pointed out that those qualities I damned in her as being late, obnoxious, disorganized, and out-of-sync with the crowd, were qualities in myself that I've fought against my whole life. This woman was reflecting back to me my own subconscious fears. With that awareness, my fear left and I could begin to see this person as a soul-like-me just trying to do the best she can. I even learned to appreciate her unique gifts.

When you accept full responsibility for life, it becomes a lot of fun. It's easy to see it in others. When President Bush is on TV railing against the "madman" Saddam Hussein, it's easy to see that Mr. Bush is really rallying against the drunken madman in himself. When the televangelist condemns homosexuality, he's really condemning his inner fear of his own homosexuality. Lo and behold, it turns out that he's a closet homosexual. The things we fight against in the world are the things we fight against in ourselves. The things we love and admire are the things we want to express more of. To be conscious and self-responsible is to accept this and view all experience as a learning opportunity for growth.

There's another aspect of being self-responsible that is often overlooked. It is to choose to be incredibly selfish. Yep, that's right, selfish. Each of us is always acting in our own perceived best self interests. Essentially, each of us is always striving to feel good. To do the best we can with the information and resources available to us at the time. Life is so simple, we just want to feel good.

There are different levels of feeling good. Some activities help us to feel good temporarily. These are gross, material, and lowercase selfish activities. Others help us to feel good for a lifetime. These are refined, *real*, and uppercase Selfish activities. On the path to enlightenment, you constantly choose those activities, people, and things that increase your capacity to feel *really* good all the time… today and forever. It is wonderful to feel good. It is the key to a life well lived. Give yourself permission to experience whatever makes you feel really good all the time. You are worth it.

The entire process of enlightening can be viewed as a progressive journey to more and more refined levels of Selfishness. As you move up the evolutionary scale, you learn to recognize, discern, and integrate finer and finer energy frequencies into your being that help you feel more safety, joy, bliss, and love all the time. Imagine feeling good all the time in any situation? It's incredibly Selfish. Jesus was Selfish. "I am Love." What an incredibly Selfish dude. Isn't that awesome? Buddha too. Imagine hanging out in Nirvana. How can you get more Selfish than that?

As you grow, you pierce the illusion of separateness. Yes, you want to be enlightened and you are making great progress. You're climbing towards the top of the mountain. As you climb your definition of Self is expanding. You see aspects of yourself in everything and everyone. You're called to reach down and help other aspects of yourself up too. From the outside looking in, it might appear that you are acting selflessly to aid and assist others. But in reality, you're doing it because it feels good to serve. Besides, you want all of your friends to come and experience this fantastic mountain high with you. Imagine hanging out with your friends and getting high all the time. Not with drugs, but from love. What a blast.

Everything you do is all done for very selfish reasons but your definition of Self is expanding to include the entire Universe. Take charity for example. At low levels of self-awareness, you might perform charity because you feel guilty or you're "supposed" to do it during the holidays. At higher levels of Self-awareness, you do it because it feels good to contribute. The first is selfish ego. The latter is Selfish spirit.

When you are self-responsible, you see the sinner and saint as the same. It's only a question of degree. It's one of refinement. Both are acting in their own perceived best self-interests, just as you are. The Yogi in the cave? A selfish dude. Mother Theresa? Incredibly selfish. Martin Luther King? Also selfish. Gandhi? Selfish. Bill Gates? Selfish. We're always looking out for our own self-interests. You, me, everyone is selfish. The only difference between Mother Theresa and Adolf Hitler is the refinement of their selfishness. Hitler saw himself as separate and superior to others. His selfishness was fear based. He was miserable. Mother Theresa saw herself as one with everyone and called to serve. Hers was love-based. Who is she serving? Even though it might appear that she is selfless, ultimately she serves herself. She was ecstatic.

It feels really good to serve from an authentic level. To serve without expectation. To make a contribution. To give freely and lovingly. Why? Because you feel love and compassion for those you serve. You see yourself and you see God reflected in everyone. You feel joy when you give. Your life is filled with meaning from an innate call to serve. On the path to enlightenment, you don't set out to change the world. You set out to feel good in the world.

As you cultivate self-responsibility, you begin to develop real compassion. Those we once judged as monsters, arrogant, or evil are reflections of our inner state. When you are self-responsible, you begin to see that everyone is doing the very best they can with the information and capabilities they have available at the time. We're all acting in our perceived best self-interest. You can now empathize with both the rapist and the victim. Both are in pain, confused, and seeking love. Both are you.

When you are self-responsible, you stop trying to change the world from the outside in. You realize that everything happening "out there" is in reality happing "in here." You look within to solve the world's problems. You seek to embody forgiveness, compassion, empathy, and understanding for you and for everyone.

As Jawaharlal Nehru, the first Prime Minister of India put it, "Peace is not a relationship of nations. It is a condition of mind brought about by a serenity of soul. Peace is not merely the absence of war. It is also a state of mind. Lasting peace can come only to peaceful people." This is self-responsibility.

Self-observation

Self-observation is the practice of observing how real-time life experiences impact your thoughts, emotions, and physical body. To be observant is to witness life unfold but not be consumed or overwhelmed by life itself. This is no easy feat.

Each of us is a unique but identical expression of the Divine. We are identical because each of us comes from something real, each of us as a soul, an intellect and ego, emotions, and physical body. We are unique only because of the cycle of action-memory-desire that constitutes a life. Allow me to explain further.

Here's a simple example of how action-memory-desire plays out in a life. There are an infinite number of these scenarios and an infinite number of variations. It is this cycle of action-memory-desire that creates our personalities and perpetuates the illusion that we are unique and separate from one another. We're all the same, we're all One--we're just running on different operating systems.

When I was a little boy of 7 or 8, I'd be alone after school until my parents came home from dinner. But some afternoons my mom would come home early from work. Those days were the best, especially when she'd make chocolate chip cookies! Walking home from the bus stop I'd wonder… was mom there? Geez, I sure hope so. Would she be baking cookies too? Oh, that would be too much to wish for. On those days when the stars were aligned, I'd walk in the back door to the kitchen and yes, my mom was there and yes, she was making cookies! That was the absolute best! She'd give me a hug and ask how my day was. The smell and anticipation of freshly baked chocolate chip cookies wafting out of the oven would fill the air. She'd bring me a plate with a glass of milk and spend time talking with me. I really felt loved! I felt alone on those days when she was working and wasn't home to greet me. Chocolate chip cookies and sugar in general became a solace for me throughout much of my life. Feeling down? Feeling lonely? Feeling stressed? Let's go find some cookies or other sweets to gorge on.

Each of us has an infinite number of these little action-memory-desire cycles playing out in our life. We are unique individuals because of this never-ending cycle. In this little scenario of mom, chocolate chip cookies, and me, the originating *action* (in an infinite stream of other actions) was coming home after school and having my mom there to greet me. This created a *memory* within me of how nice it was to have my mom home after school. At some point, my mom had to work and stopped being there after school. In turn, this triggered a *desire* within me to have my mom there, especially when I was having a bad day.

Sometimes my mom would bake chocolate chip cookies, creating a new *action* and a new *memory* within me. This in turn created a new *desire* to have my mom and my cookies too. Occasionally, my mom wouldn't be there after school but she'd still make me chocolate chip cookies. Having the cookies but not my mom, created a new *action* and a new *memory* of cookies as a sort of surrogate for my mom. Later in life, if I was engaged in actions that made me feel low and let down, I'd trigger my now subconscious memory of solace from my mom which transferred to another suitable female, chocolate chip cookies and sugar, and whoa, would I have a burning *desire* to get some love through sugar.

For someone else, perhaps an action was reaching a hand in the cookie jar only to be smacked upside the head from their mom for stealing. We're always seeking pleasure and avoiding pain. This action created an unpleasant memory, which in turn creates new desires to take new actions. There's an infinite number of new actions to take here for any individual… avoid cookies, avoid stealing, consume cookies guiltily, steal for love and attention... whatever.

This constantly spinning cycle of action-memory-desire creates strong neural and biophysical patterns within each of us. Our perceived individuality is really just this little software program constantly running in the background. It's happening so fast that most of us are only vaguely aware of it and then only at certain times. Most of us just operate unconsciously from this software of the soul.

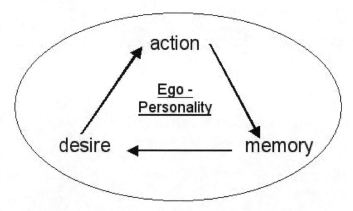

Figure 4. The software of the soul creates our personality, ego, and perpetuates the illusion that we are separate.

As you engage in self-observation, you are slowly and surely breaking these unconscious patterns and establishing new more conscious ones. A superior new pattern is one that isn't even a pattern at all. It is a non-pattern that allows more reality to shine through. You break the cycle of action-memory-desire altogether and bask in reality. It's like you're a computer hacker who hacks into the mainframe software operating system, removes it, and replaces it with an entirely new one that gives new superior levels of performance.

To conceptualize how the cycle of action-memory-desire fits into your life experience, picture a tall pyramid as a metaphor for your life. The pyramid is divided into three sections, a base, middle, and top.

The top of the pyramid is the world of form. Here is the matter and energy that comprise the physical universe. At this level you can perceive your body and other interesting forms such as girlfriends, boyfriends, puppies, butterflies, planets, solar systems, light waves, gravity, and all the matter and energy that makes up the physical world. This is the world of effects and conditions. But they're all created and caused by the deeper layers of the pyramid below.

The middle of the pyramid is subtler. Here lies your mind, or emotions, intellect, and soul as well as the seat for the action-memory-desire cycle. This subtler world gives rise to the form at the top of the pyramid above. What you believe, unconsciously or consciously, is held here and gives rise to your experiences in the world above. As you believe, so it is. Here too resides your personality and ego, created through the cycle of action-memory-desire. Your ego tends to attach itself to the objects of its experience. Things like "my car" "my wife" "my job". You know from experience that there's great pain involved when the ego gets too attached to these objects and they don't act as expected.

The base of the pyramid is the widest and deepest. Your true power resides here and gives form and function to the rest of the pyramid above. At this level is your direct connection the one Universal Source, Spirit, or God. This is the level of first cause. Here is your baseline, your connection to the One real source that gives rise to everything else in the Universe. The closer you can get to this reality, the more blissful, powerful, aware, and in the flow your life is. The only thing that prevents this reality from fully shining forth is your old software programming, the rapid and often unconscious cycle of action-memory-desire.

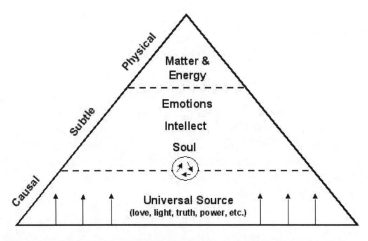

Figure 5. The light of reality shines forth fully in your life once your false conditioning, the old action-memory-desire cycle, stops spinning so rapidly and unconsciously.

To be self-observant is to practice witnessing this software cycle of action-memory-desire in real-time through your life. By observing it, and following the other practices of self-responsibility, reflection, release and support, you begin to re-write your programming and allow the light of Spirit to shine through with brilliance.

An authentic practice is one that allows you to become more aware of the cycle running in your life, observe it, reflect on it, and release it so that it is naturally replaced with more light, love, truth, and beauty.

As your development progresses, you become aware of more subtle undulations in your being. You start to become highly in tune with your own physical, mental, emotional, and subtler forms. You become highly aware of other people and energies around you.

What's happening in the moment right now? Is my breathing deep or shallow? Is my gut twingy or at peace? Is my mind racing or quiet? How do I feel? Will this food best support me right now? Or am I acting out of a habit? You become a highly observant being of yourself and others.

You don't go overboard with observation. You're not constantly psychoanalyzing yourself, consumed entirely with your inner world. Actually, what happens by virtue of your practice is that you become a finely tuned instrument that is keenly aware of what's happening within you and around you without even spending much time thinking about it.

Your primary observation point is placed upon how you're feeling inside. You have a base line of authentic feeling. It's your connection to reality within, your Authentic Self. As you progress up the evolutionary spiral, this baseline increases in power and scope. You become more and more aware of what it's like to reside there. It feels really, really good to be in this connection. The distractions of the outer world become less and less distracting. As you get familiar with this place, it becomes easier to tell when you're operating unconsciously, running on some tired old software programming.

It's easy to tell because you don't feel as good anymore. You've lost your baseline connection. You went unconscious. That good feeling is gone. You've switched from a love-based being mode to a fear-based doing mode. That's OK, no problem. You just observe what caused the fall-off and bring your attention back to God within. The more you reconnect, the easier it is to bring your awareness back home.

One self-observation practice I enjoy and that I've found to be incredibly valuable to illuminate and reinforce my process of observation is journaling.

By journaling each morning, I consciously review and observe my day before. What was the big learning of yesterday? How was my energy? How was my use of time? How did my diet serve me? How was my connection to Source? When did it increase? When was I unconscious? As I write my journal, addressing these and other questions, I gain insight into what's contributing to my self-realization and what's not. I can then choose to make new choices that better serve my growth. What can be learned here? What can be transformed? What can be accepted? What is the message? It's very powerful and transformative stuff.

As I write this book, I'm aware that my growth edge is consciously spending more and more time in joyful connection with my Authentic Self. I have become a highly observant dude of others and myself. Even so, I still find myself falling off regularly throughout my day. My baseline is bliss. But I can get caught up in action mode, running unconsciously. I feel time pressure, I worry about how to do something, fears come up. Relationships and experiences all unfold in my external environment and can temporarily overpower my connection and knock me off of my game. I go unconscious.

It's OK, I notice when I'm off more and more. I tell myself, "Thank God for showing me where I am not yet free." It's easier for me to come back faster and faster. This is the dance, an evolving progression.

I imagine that to be fully self-realized is to hardly ever have a thought or a moment of unconsciousness. It's to reside fully and completely as your Authentic Self everywhere, all the time, and in all situations. This is my commitment. This is my practice. This is my growth edge. What is yours?

Self-reflection

The practices of self-responsibility and observation provide a life buoy in the sea of change. Consider them essential maintenance and development activities. But to make great strides in your evolution you also need to take time out from day-to-day activities and allow the light of reality to fully shine forth. It is reflection that deepens, broadens, and strengthens your connection to God within. By reflecting on Truth, you are able to reveal more Truth in your life.

I reflect for at least an hour a day, every day, in meditation. I think this is the minimum amount for anyone engaged on the path, It's my favorite time of day. What am I reflecting on? I'm reflecting on the Spirit within me. I just sit in meditation and allow that light, that life force of reality, to shine forth within me, through me, and as me. It feels so incredible to simply sit and bask in God's light, love, and grace. Wow.

Meditation is an essential self-reflection practice. Every enlightened master, ancient and new, from every tradition has spent considerable amounts of time in meditation. But as Lama Thubten Yeshe a Tibetan monk put it, "Whether we sit with our arms folded this way and our legs crossed that way is of little consequence. But it is extremely important to check and see if whatever meditation we do is an actual remedy for our suffering."

I couldn't agree more. There are many ways to meditate. Each has its own path, its own rhythm and experience. Meditation unfolds in a sequence, but the specific experiences and unfolding vary from person to person and from method to method. What method is right for you? You'll find it. Just be open about it. Don't tie yourself religiously to one technique. Keep in mind that the goal is to reveal more reality, more love, light, and truth in your life. To become free.

There are wonderful techniques and you can choose what feels right for you from all traditions and cultures. Try those that resonate with you personally. Practice them sincerely to see what results you experience. Find those that work best. It is just not possible to chart a single path, or to say that every individual will have the same experience with any given technique. The paths of the mind, the heart, and the body will each take you there. But one clear path will eventually open up for you. When you find it, you'll know it. Your journey and progress begins to radically accelerate. The technique just feels so right for *you*.

Ram Dass, in his book Journey to Awakening, captures the balance well. He writes, "I've found that each meditation technique I've ever pursued seriously has helped me by touching another space in my being. Somehow I've danced through them without getting caught in a value system that would say that a single meditative technique is the only way. You cannot, however, keep collecting methods all the way to enlightenment. Sooner or later you will be drawn to one path or another, which is for you the eye of the needle, the doorway to the inner temple. The journey passes from eclectic sampling to a single path. Finally, you recognize the unity of your own way and that of other seekers who followed other paths. At the peak, all paths come together."

So yes, absolutely meditate. You're not meditating for any flashy experience. You're meditating to reflect the God within you more clearly, more brilliantly, more lovingly to yourself. You meditate to perceive more reality. You reveal by yourself for yourself that everything is within you, every atom of the Universe, and that you already embody perfection from within.

In addition to meditation, some of my greatest evolutionary leaps have occurred in retreat settings. A retreat is a deep period of reflection. Something magical happens when I put myself into a sacred space joined by fellow seekers on the path and guided by authentic leaders. A retreat immerses me in the experience of transformation. It provides access to new levels of self-discovery and unleashes tremendous amounts of untapped energy. In the dozens of retreats I've experienced, from a variety of different traditions and practices, I've never had a bad experience. In fact, I've always had an awesome one. The new tools I pick up, new spiritual friends, the learning, the growth, and increased awareness are all priceless.

There's a season to grow and a season to reap. The season to grow is a period of self-reflection. If life is a mirror then when we practice self-reflection we clean the mirror. We transform the self-limiting beliefs and habits that prevent our real light from shining forth. A retreat setting occurs when we take time, it could be as short as a day, from the noise, distraction, and accelerated pace of daily living. Time to sit deeply in meditation, to pray, to be in silence, to inquire on the nature of ourselves and our purpose on this planet.

As we come out of retreat, the journey continues, we continue to practice self-responsibility, observation, reflection, release and support. But now we're able to do it from a new level of self-awareness. Perhaps we have even acquired new tools for our personal development tool kit as well. Now we're reaping. This is all good stuff.

A retreat period of deep self-reflection allows you to climb higher and reach new peaks in your evolution. You self-reflect and increase your carrying capacity for love. You go back into the world and this awareness tends to fade. But you've stretched and expanded your carrying capacity. You can fill this new capacity with more love as you continue to practice.

Self-release

Self-release is to love, accept, and forgive all aspects of you just as you are. There are parts of you that you judge, condemn, or unconsciously cling to. There are many false traps that your conditioned self will seek out to feel good. At the same time, you recognize that this old conditioning doesn't really serve you any more. Power? Money? Indulgence? Intoxication? Security? Judgment? Anger? Addiction? Food? Relationships? We tell ourselves that it's just "Who I am," or "I want it, I like it," or "I can't help myself." But afterwards we feel less than good. Feelings of guilt, remorse, sadness, or recrimination cloud our perception.

This negative conditioning is actually wonderful. It provides the impetus to change. When you're disgusted, angry, or fearful of some part of you, you begin the process of opening to change. "I'm so sick and tired of this same old pattern, I'm going to do something about it once and for all." Have you ever found yourself saying that?

Early in my process I was motivated to hunt down and try to kill all the negative conditioning within me. I had patterns and I was sick of them. I was ready and willing to go deep within, find them, and destroy them.

"Ah-ha, I've got you now you bastard! You're mine."

I believed that with enough awareness and will power, I would finally be free. If I could find the pattern and shine a light on it, I told myself, then I would be rid of it once and for all. With enough awareness, dedication, and courage, I would finally win.

Did it work? No! Trying to locate and hunt negative conditioning within yourself is like being Elmer Fudd hunting Bugs Bunny. You are never going to catch the rabbit this way.

In actuality, my desire to find and get rid of my perceived negative conditioning was just another dance with my ego. I'd spot the pattern, discover it, and try to conquer it. I was in a great battle with my self. Time and again though, the old pattern would come rushing back into my life, usually right when I felt like I had it beat once and for all.

"Damn, I did it again." Then I go in search for the underlying reason only to rediscover the same old legacy pattern in a new light. I'd feel dejected and discouraged. "Man, I'm never going to beat this thing. It's hopeless."

Here's the thing. I was battling myself for self-mastery. It's a can't-win situation and a classic trap. It's a trap the ego loves to play because it maintains control. Whatever we repress in life eventually gets expressed. You can't fight your way through to self-realization. You can't beat, fight, or condemn things out of yourself.

The secret is to love and accept all aspects of you. *All* aspects. Even the ones you find distasteful, abhorrent, weak, and despicable. The kinds of deep, dark, wretched places that you don't want anyone to really know about. Not even you. By cultivating love and compassion for yourself, including your unconscious patterns, you're finally able to release anything and everything that is preventing your fullest embodiment of self-realization.

This can be a little tricky. Yes, you want to release your negative patterns. But you can't actually release them. In fact, by even trying to release them, you end up clinging to them. Instead, you've got to *not* want to clear them and clear them all at the same time. Tricky, I know. You've got to want to embrace them, love them, and feel so much love and compassion for them that you weep. It's through love and compassion that you transform your inner hurts and fears. You are releasing any of the gunk and goop that is preventing you from living life at your highest potential by loving and accepting everything and anything about you. Like everything else in spiritual growth, it becomes its own paradox.

So what do you need to release? Here's the key when it comes to identifying what to release and let go in your life. Does it feel deeply good while you're doing it and after you've done it too? If it only feels good while you do it, then it's an addiction. If it feels good while you do it, after you do it, and adds to your overall sense of inner peace and well being, that's the ticket.

Be gentle with yourself in releasing the things that you can't seem to shake. Learn to cultivate compassion and acceptance of your negative conditioning. Then go even further. Celebrate it. Identify how it has contributed to your growth. Without the pain and anguish, you'd never evolve. There is no part of you that is wrong, bad, unworthy, or evil. You are perfect, timeless, loving, whole, creative, and real. As you release, you're letting go of false misperceptions. You are embracing more reality. You are increasing your carrying capacity to handle more love and more compassion.

This increase in carrying capacity will likely freak you out at first. Sometimes it can even feel too intense. It's uncomfortable at times to consciously carry new and higher frequencies of energy. You might find yourself running back to old and "safe" patterns to decrease the flow of Source in your life. If this happens, don't condemn and don't judge. Accept and love yourself as you cultivate compassion for your behavior. Cultivate compassion for your mind, emotions, and body. You're on the warriors' path and all warriors need love, compassion, and acceptance. This is the gateway.

As you practice compassion and empathy for yourself, this compassion naturally extends to others. In fact, without love and compassion for yourself first, you are incapable of true compassion and care for others. Life is lived inside out. By practicing love and compassion, you release your fears and unconscious conditioning. You transform what is false into what is real. Your loving nature extends and expands to embrace everyone and everything you come in contact with. Guess what? You are self-releasing the old and making way for the new.

Self-support

I'm of the opinion that no one can make this journey alone. Each of us needs lots of love and support. This is good. It's fun to do the work with others. It's wonderful to receive and it's wonderful to give. Giving and receiving are two sides of the same coin. By opening yourself up to receive support, you allow others to experience more of their own self-realization through service and contribution. We're all in this together. Our journeys are different but also the same. We choose different paths but ultimately all end up at the same destination.

When it comes to self-support, begin with how you treat yourself. Develop a mindset that allows you to receive good, blessings, and support from the Universe. Be good to yourself. Be open to receive. Allow others to share their gifts with you. Get a massage. Get a facial. Go to a course. Visit the beach. Have fun all the time. Ask for assistance. Just allow the Universe to support you unconditionally, because it will.

Specifically to self-evolution, there are four things that I've found to be invaluable to support my journey along the path, get unstuck, and make monumental leaps forward. They are 1) mentoring/coaching, 2) a like-minded spiritual community, 3) a spiritual teacher, and 4) support to stay grounded.

Working with a one-to-one mentor or coach has been very valuable to transform information in my head into living wisdom in my heart. There's just something about the power of human-to-human connection when I'm encouraged to express what new information means to me and how it relates to my ideas, values, and commitments. When I talk it through, I make it real. Something magical happens during a coaching session. My coach has no other agenda than my progression. They don't want anything from me or need anything from me. It's a free and safe sounding board to explore, try on, and grow. Often times what I think is the issue in my life isn't really the issue at all and that only reveals itself while being coached. Every great artist, athlete, entertainer, statesman, author, business person, and parent has a least one coach. Is your life worthy of the same care and respect? You bet it is.

A good coach does two other things really well; he or she helps you to recognize and accept responsibly as well as frame and ask the right questions.

It is so easy to spot things in others. It is so easy to point the finger of blame and responsibility elsewhere. It is significantly more challenging to spot responsibility in us. We've discussed how each of us is 100% responsible for our life conditions and experiences. I tell you what, there are certain things I attract in my life and I have no idea why. I am absolutely flummoxed as to my own responsibility. In fact, I doubt that I am even partly responsible, even though I know better. But when I get together with one of my coaches, they help me to uncover my own responsibility. The light bulb goes off and now I can choose to change. A good coach is an expert at helping you uncover your blind spots. They excel at helping you accept responsibility.

A coach is also an expert at helping to frame and ask the right questions, questions that inspire and uplift you to new and better inner answers. The process of asking sound questions is the foundation of personal evolution. It all starts with the questions and a good coach will make sure you're asking the best questions of yourself.

I also encourage you to get involved with a like-minded spiritual community. There is great support in this domain. I spent most of my journey as a free agent. Church and organized religion was anathema to me. But just recently I came across a group of like-minded people at a trans-denominational spiritual center near my home.

Wow. Was I missing out all those years! I totally love it. It's a chance to go each week, participate with others, and raise my frequency. I tell you what, the energy of this little spiritual center will knock your socks off. It's a total blast. It aligns with my personal philosophy. There's no hypocrisy between the theology and my beliefs. I've learned a lot. I get to bring my kids and introduce them to the same concepts I've fallen in love with. There's a sense of community, affinity, and home. I am so grateful for this spiritual center. If you don't have a place like this, I encourage you to open to the possibilities. I'm so glad I did. I didn't realize how much I missed the feeling of community until I found it again.

The third area of support is to be in the presence of a spiritual teacher. A spiritual teacher is different than a coach or a mentor. This is a person who has gone very, very far in his or her own evolution. They embody what it means to be enlightened. They transmit the frequency of love by their very presence. You evolve just by being in their presence. My current teacher has spent years and years in dedicated spiritual practice and let me tell you, the energy I receive is awesome!

My American mindset was not very comfortable working with a teacher or guru (guru means one who teaches). But in most parts of the world, a teacher-student relationship is the proven path to self-realization. It's not conducted out of superiority. It's conducted out of love and recognition that all is One. If you help me raise my vibration, then I naturally raise your vibration too. In just a few weeks of working with a dedicated teacher I radically shifted the caliber of my vibration. But I'm a good student! I ask sincere questions, I'm committed to my self-realization, and I practice diligently. It's like everything else in life. You get out of it what you put into it, but a guru, by their very presence, can accelerate your progression rapidly.

There is one other dimension of support to consider. It's not support to help you go forward, it's support to keep you from flying away! As you move forward in your evolution, you're going to be carrying much higher frequencies in your being. This flow of reality needs to be managed or it can become overpowering and uncomfortable. Breath work, exercise, yoga asanas, acupuncture, loving sex, coaching, a teacher, deep listening, and heart-felt conversation, are all sound practices to help release too much energy, just as they work to increase your energy. I've known people whose hair has fallen out while in the process of learning to handle more love and reality. I've had friends tell me they have found themselves levitating right off the floor.

It's not to be taken lightly, but at the same time, you are already a divine being of light and power. You are already realized. Be clear on your intentions and commitment to experience more realization naturally, effortlessly, and perfectly and the support you need will always be there for you.

So this is the practice of self-realization. You started out in fear, shame, guilt, and recrimination. You practice accepting and liberating yourself with higher and higher doses of love, compassion, and forgiveness. Your continued practice of Self-responsibility, Self-reflection, Self-observation, Self-release and Self-support allows your evolution to unfold naturally. Lots of things change with your practice. How you perceive the world, how you perceive yourself, and how you perceive God. But the basic questions remain the same: What's in it for me? Who am I? And how far can I go?

The more you discern your higher Self interests, the more capacity you have to carry these higher energies and the higher you go. This is the practice of self-realization. After some time with consistent and diligent practice, you will be prepared for the final great leap--the step of surrender.

Five questions to ponder regarding your practice…

1. What are my current spiritual practices? How are they serving me? Are there any not serving me?

2. How responsible am I being with my life?

3. How observant am I of my thoughts and feelings? How do I know when I'm connected and when I'm not?

4. What do I need to release from my life? What do I need to accept and embrace?

5. What support will help me get to where I really want to be?

Surrender

"Love is a lot like dancing-you just surrender to the music."

--Anonymous

The final step of enlightenment is to surrender your life completely to God. This isn't done on faith. It's not done out of fear or because your guru told you to. It's done out of love because you want to. Nothing else matters. Nothing else even comes close.

To surrender is to willingly, lovingly, and expectantly turn everything in your life over to what's real. At this stage, you never want to think another thought, have another desire, and speak another word that doesn't come directly from your Authentic Self. You know this part of you to be real. You want full-time, all-the-time communion with it. You're willing to give up everything and anything to have it. It's your highest goal.

All of your previous steps on the journey make this final step both possible and desired. You literally want to turn everything in your life over to God. You plead to turn it over. You bow down in utter humility to turn it over. You affirm to turn it over. You just want out of your head, you want out of your small misconceptions of who you are and what you're here for. You just simply want to bask fully, completely, all the time, and in every situation in the glory of God--that singular real place residing within you, of you, around you, and everything else in the Universe.

God is Real. It is. God is Life. God is All. You want to be more real. Your soul is bursting to be one with reality. That's where you belong because that's who you are. You are going home.

> "I surrender everything fully and completely to God. I open totally to reality and I allow it to be so. God think through me, feel through me, speak through me and direct me. I willingly and joyfully turn my entire life over. Guide me to be a pure vehicle of divine love, light, and wisdom. I want to remember what is real, everywhere, all the time, and in every situation. Thank God!"

The dance doesn't end at surrender. You keep progressing and you keep evolving. You keep asking new questions, recommitting, practicing, and surrendering. But surrender is where you make the big leaps in consciousness. The more you are able to surrender, the faster you progress.

Being ready and willing to surrender your life to God is so far distant from where you began that it's almost indescribable. How did you get here? Before surrendering, you can look back at your evolutionary progress and realize that your desire, your commitment to transform has accelerated your growth and brought you very far. Your constant practice of becoming more real, using whatever methods seem most powerful to you, has enabled great strides. Enlightenment has become your highest goal. You're working hard for it. You're familiar with various practices, theories, and techniques to practice. You've sought answers, teachers, guidance and support. You're doing all the things you're "supposed" to do.

Yes, you've made and are making great progress. Yes, you're having peak experiences of joy, bliss, and transcendence. Yes, you understand that you create your own life, that you are timeless, boundless, and eternal at your core. And when you're having an off day, when life seems to be hitting you really hard between the eyes, you know what to do to get out of it and very frequently do.

But eventually, there arise some burdens that just feel too heavy to carry. They weigh on your soul. You are trying so hard to transcend your fears, doubts, and self-limitations. You want love, joy, and bliss so badly. You are committed, you practice, and it's your highest goal. But something or someone or some pattern keeps showing up in your life that causes you great pain. You just can't seem to let it go, to get out of your own way. It really, really hurts. It's almost as if he, she, or it keeps showing up to point out exactly where you still have fear, pain, sadness, grief, and vulnerability in your life. Here, take this knife and jab it in my heart.

There is a purpose to this pain, suffering, and depression. You're learning to surrender to God. You're learning to let go of everything you think your life should be, of how you want things to be, and turn it all over. Before surrender, it's as if the Universe is conspiring to beat out everything and anything within you that is in the way of your highest good.

The Universe wants the very best for you. It has a grand and marvelous plan for you that you co-create and shape. When you're not listening, when you're fighting and trying to control how things should be, you're beating your head against an unstoppable force. This is the pain you're feeling. Eventually, you'll get so worn down, so exasperated and frustrated that you'll just stop fighting and struggling. You stop clinging to how you think you want something to be and make space for the Universe to reveal its grandiosity.

You've fought this final transformation because you've defined yourself through whatever it is that's blocking it. We all hold on to things outside ourselves that we believe bring us happiness. We cling to a marriage, a relationship, a job, an income, a status, something. They all keep their hold on us. We'll fight to the death to keep them. We rationalize. We bargain.

"Hey, I have a good marriage. If you're asking me to give that up, screw you. I don't want enlightenment at that price." Or,

"I've worked thirty years on my business. I'm successful. People are counting on me. I'm not just going to give it up."

I'm not saying that you're going to have to give those things up. In actuality, at higher levels of realization, the relationships, activities and material things you currently appreciate in your life will take on added meaning, richness, joy, and satisfaction. Moreover, despite what you've given up, your entire life will radically and immeasurably improve beyond description. Everything becomes much easier. What I'm saying is this: You've got to be *willing* to give it up. You've got to be willing to turn everything in your life over to God within you and as you. Not in an apathetic way. Not in a "Oh, God give me mercy" way. You do it in a conscious and loving way. You do it with faith and trust.

Your steps of asking, committing, and practicing are progressing. You're performing them all the time. You commit each day to realize the full expression of you. You practice being more real all the time. You meditate, pray, do yoga, and exercise. You surround yourself with support. You get coaching, receive bodywork, eat foods that nourish you, join groups and communities. You find avenues for service, express your joy, fall off the wagon, journal, learn, observe, and grow. You recognize and accept that the trials that emerge are all for your highest good and evolution.

Finally, all of your efforts up to this point have in reality made you feel safe enough in your relationship with God to fully, willingly, and joyfully turn everything over. It's like watching a new birth, the re-birth of a soul. It is so achingly beautiful that I weep with joy just thinking about it.

On my own progression, I was trying so hard to arrive. I was studying, learning, sifting, sorting, trying to make sense of everything that self-realization should be. I was trying to find the very best practice, the very best methods to accelerate my growth. This desire, this hard work, this need to know and make sense of it all was actually weighing me down. It was like I was carrying around a 100-pound backpack in my head. I thought I knew what enlightenment should be. All of this hard work was necessary for me. It got me to the final step of surrender.

I wanted greater self-realization but on my own conditions. There were some things I wasn't willing to bargain with. One of them was my business. I was engaged in this personal transformation effort so that I could be a better CEO. So that I could manage my businesses in a new and innovative way and at the same time, enjoy my life to the fullest. Several years ago, I felt called to launch a new venture that would combine my talents for creativity, communication, and teaching with my newfound discoveries in personal transformation. But not only that, I was committed to prove a new way of doing business; one that focused not only on profit but also on people, planet, and making a positive contribution.

I created the world's first distance learning and integrated life coaching platform. I didn't just want to communicate ideas; I wanted to change people's lives. I spent a fortune on it. I hired up, took office space, and paid a team from India to develop the platform from the ground up. I was totally confident that it was going to be a smash hit. After all, look at the benefits I was experiencing. The local beta test also revealed very positive, life changing results for our clients. I had great dreams for the business. It would be my vehicle to make a meaningful contribution, do what I thought I loved to do, and make money all at the same time. Secretly inside I was saying, "God is calling me to do this. God wants me to do it. I'm aligned with Source and I'm committed. Look out world, here I come."

Crash! The business was a total failure. I couldn't get customers to engage. I mortgaged the house. Went as far as I could and kaput. Nothing. Stress. Fear. Failure. All of it shot to the surface. It was a very, very trying time. And I was seething.

"What kind of bullshit was this? Didn't I do everything I was supposed to do? Didn't I follow my life purpose and passion and take mighty risks? You bet I did and look what I got. A mortgaged house, failed business, disappointed employees, and an angry, resentful wife. What the fuck did I sign up for?"

I went through the long, arduous process of closing it down. I accepted various consulting jobs to pay the bills. I went to work for two of my mentors. I felt small, dejected, and abandoned by God. I could only see other people's success around me. None of it my own. I spent several months oscillating back and forth through the classic stages of loss--denial, anger, bargaining, and depression. Finally, I got to a place of acceptance. With acceptance comes space and I was able to reflect on the entire experience and understand the final step of surrender.

As I reflected on my experience, I got in touch with some very important transformative lessons. First, I was able to recognize that I started the business so that I could prove I was "good enough." That same old pattern had never left me. It runs deep and I was covering it up.

"Look world, look how good I am? Can't you see how hard I'm trying? Can't you see all the sacrifices I'm making? Look God, now can you let me in? Look--look how much better and different I'm doing it over here? Please, please can I be safe now? Can I be loved now?"

The layers of the onion run very, very deep. The vestiges of this old pattern still lingered.

Second, I realized my greatest fear--failure in my chosen field. Failure to me was more terrifying then death. Failure meant shame, grief, and ridicule. It confirmed that I wasn't really good enough. Now I know that you're supposed to view failure as a stepping stone--that great mistakes lead to great victories and all that stuff but that's not how I carried failure. It was debilitating. It was humiliating. Well guess what? It wasn't nearly as bad as I thought it would be. In fact, it was no big deal. I was afraid of a paper tiger. I failed at a new business and the world still continues to spin on its axis. Liberating.

Third, I gained a tremendous amount of appreciation for how I tricked myself into self-awakening. You see, I defined myself as an entrepreneur. I began my quest for self-realization to pick up some new tools and techniques so that I could do it better. With this false armor of entrepreneurship, I began to research new and innovative things. I guarantee that unless I had the badge of "business research" on my chest, I never would have done these things. There's no way I would have ever mustered the courage to go to a seminar or to study cutting edge thought unless I had convinced myself that it was to turn it into a business of some kind. I would never have spent the money unless I thought it was going to come back. The guise of an entrepreneur doing business research made it safe enough for me to go out in the world and explore. The guise was so good I didn't even know I was wearing it!

And as I reflected on these epiphanies and transformations, something else really struck me. I actually got everything that I was searching for when I set out on my quest. It just wasn't delivered how I expected it to be. I sat down and made a list of all the things I had received from my process of waking up. It was both humbling and awe inspiring. Sure, a business failed but the benefits were truly priceless. Here's the list I wrote:

- Constant connection with my Source
- Hugely expanded Self-awareness
- Increased intuition, creativity, and knowingness
- Experience of regular peak and transcendent experiences
- Freedom to express what's in my heart
- Regular feelings of bliss, wonder, and joy
- Accepting responsibility for my life
- Detached observance of my thoughts and feelings
- Increase of my inner power

- Greater feelings of safety and security
- Learning and growing more each day
- Intimate relationships and friendships
- Laughter at the whole play

Later on, while writing this book actually, I recognized something else about this experience of business loss. As I reflect on that period, I don't believe that I was really listening to the vision and direction my Authentic Self was providing. True, I was kind of sort of listening. I was kind of sort of following. But I was doing it on my ego's terms and conditions. I wasn't playing flat out. In a way, I was cheating.

You see, throughout my quest, every time I asked, "What should I do with my life to be happy, prosperous, and fulfilled?" the answer I got back from my Authentic Self was very simple: Transform yourself through love and teach--share your experience with others. Sometimes it was like a mantra in my head. Transform and teach. Transform and teach. Transform and teach. But every time I heard it, I denied it. I denied it in a myriad of ways.

At first, I denied it by saying this: "No, not that. I'm not a teacher. I'm an entrepreneur. I'm a business person. I want to make a lot of money. I want to run a large company. Maybe then I can teach. Besides, I don't have any credibility. Who would believe anything I have to say? I'm an unknown. I have no degree. I have no qualifications."

Then over several years, through my searching, seeking, and transformation, I began to feel more credible. I still didn't have a teaching degree, but my inward view of myself had shifted. By virtue of my first-hand experience, I now felt credible. 'Lo and behold,' I thought, 'I actually do have things to teach.' I now felt the confidence that I previously lacked.

I'd ask again, "What should I do with my life?" Again, the same response, "Transform yourself and teach what you know to be true." OK, I thought, I'm finally ready now. I'm going to follow this signal. I'm going to commit and trust and play flat out. I'm going to transform and teach to the best of my ability.

But did I? Sort of. The idea of stepping out and teaching was still terrifying to me. I pooh-poohed those who were doing it. Write a book? No thanks, any schmuck can write a book. Coaching others one at a time? Too boring. I'll teach and transform but I need to do it in an innovative and big way.

But my innovative approach was really just another cover. I was scared to fully step out, be fearless and do what I was deeply called to do, operating from right where I was. My innovative web site design and distance learning and life coaching platform was really a big and expensive excuse for me to say that I was stepping out but like the Wizard of Oz, still remain hidden behind the curtain. I was following my calling but not to the fullest extent of my capabilities.

There's a classic life question that flits around the personal development space, "If you absolutely knew you could not fail, what would you do with your life?" My answer is that I would write books, give talks, coach others, and participate in creative new ventures that make a positive difference on the planet… all the while transforming myself and teaching others. Was I doing that with this venture? I thought so at the time but in hindsight, I don't think I really was. It was as far as I could stretch at the time. But it was all a big cover to protect my ego from its fear of being seen and judged as not good enough.

I think God wants more from me. God wants more from you too. God wants the full, fearless, divine expression from each of us. That place within you that is both terrifying and liberating. God wants you to play flat out for that deep resonant call inside of you. God wants you to go for it and step fully into your divine talents and truthful expression. Halfway measures aren't going to cut it. The pain will persist as long as the vision resists. The Authentic Self must express itself fully. This is the vision. What would you do if you absolutely knew you could not fail?

And this leads me to the act of surrender. I had tried so hard to do what I thought was right. I was trying so hard to be "good enough" and to fulfill my mission and purpose in life. I finally realized, through this business failure, and my corresponding increase in Self-awareness that I was already good enough. I was already whole, perfect, and infinite at my real core. My journey to more self-realization began in crisis and it ended in crisis but this second crisis was very, very different than the first.

I was finally ready to get completely out of my own way. I was ready to really listen to that still, small voice within. I was ready to finally be fearless in my commitment. Why was I trying to run my life from my small brain when I had direct access to so much love and wisdom? Why was I still trying to control things to how I thought they should be? What was I afraid of really? I was ready to surrender. I was finally ready to make the ultimate leap.

But even this ultimate leap is an illusion. There's no drama, no risk in surrender other than what you create in your own mind. Everything in your life is already an aspect of God so there's nothing really to surrender to. You are already realized. The only thing you're giving up is your desire to control things the way your ego wants them to be.

Before surrender, in effect, you're saying this: "Yes, I want enlightenment but only on these conditions: I also want to keep my marriage, my job, my health, and my finances stable or improving. I want happiness but not at the expense of these things. Moreover, here's what I think enlightenment should be like (after all, I've studied it and envisioned it) and so I'd like it to appear like this." It's these conditions that we place on our evolution, often times unconscious, that create the pain and suffering we're experiencing. The stronger the grip, the deeper the pain in letting go.

This is a battle you cannot win. The preconditions you cling to create the suffering you experience. At some point, through trial, tragedy, or you just get smart enough, you'll want to surrender it all to God. This is when you are finally ready to trust fully in Divine Intelligence. You have a deep understanding of God, of how the Source expresses purely through you, of how your mind and preconditions cannot compete with the pure good, perfection, and harmony of the Universe, so why are you struggling to have things your way? Ultimately, you surrender. You realize that you are one with God, within God and as God, that God has your very best interests at heart. That God, who infinitely orchestrates the entire Universe perfectly, wants you to evolve. You ask, you allow, you are open to receive the love of God. You desire to turn everything in your life over to God. Through grace, you are elevated.

Wow, this is an exhilarating leap. It becomes the ultimate commitment and the ultimate practice. You recognize the reality of God and that's where you want to reside. This is the final step of enlightenment. Surrender. Release. Let go. Allow God to handle everything. You continue to commit to your highest evolution. You continue to practice being more real using your favorite practices and techniques. But now, once you've surrendered, you do it all in a celebration of God's love. Your only true desire in life is to walk with God, talk with God, and be with God all the time. Why? Because it is real. Because you are in awe, ineffability, and humility, of the expanse, power, and love of God. Surrender. Let go.

The American philosopher Ernest Holmes captures the essence of the desire and act of surrender so beautifully in this written meditation.

Peace is the Power at the Heart of God

My peace is found at the heart of God. The heart of God, for me is found at the very center of my being. It does not matter how closely the confusion of the outer world presses against me, I am not even disturbed by the confusion in my immediate environment. I know that the only way to counteract confusion is to bring peace into play. "Peace I leave with you, my peace I give unto you; not as the world giveth, give I unto you." These words of assurance stay with me, and I hear them re-echoing in the depths of my being.

I surrender all of my fears--those nameless fears which have beset me for such a long time, dulling my pleasure and clouding with misery and apprehension all of my days. I am now through with fear. What, indeed is there for a divine and immortal being to fear. Certainly not people, for as I am a divine and immortal being, so is every man and every man is my brother. I recognize the one Life Principle, working in and through and inspiring the motives of everyone I contact.

I do not fear sickness, disease or death, because the eternal and perfect Life animates my body and goes always about its perfect work, healing and renewing that body. I am not afraid of want or lack, for the one infinite Essence supplies me with everything I need all of the time. There is nothing for me to fear, for I am an inseparable part of God. I live in Him; He lives in me; and I draw upon His perfect peace.

The act of surrender, just like questioning, commitment, and practice, is done in stages. You stretch yourself. Life gives you challenges and lessons for growth. You learn to do each one a little bit better, to let go a little bit more. These things set the framework for your entire existence. You are committed to realizing the full expression of you and to fulfill your life's contribution. You practice being a pure expression of the Divine all the time. You seek a clear and unobstructed channel with Source and so you practice clearing, deepening, and enlivening that connection. You surrender to God. You let go of fear. You let go of false desires. You let go of false perceptions. You see and feel your Universal connection with all things and recognize that you and everything are the same. It's all a unique expression of the same Divine source. You see this, feel this, and are one with this Source. This is the process of self-realization. Now you are flying.

Five questions to ponder regarding your surrender…

1. Who or what is God? Is it safe to surrender to God?

2. What aspects of my life am I still trying to control?

3. What am I willing to give up in order to have enlightenment?

4. How does God reveal itself in my life today?

5. What fears keep me from surrendering completely?

Putting It All Together

"All the art of living lies in a fine mingling of letting go and holding on."

--Havelock Ellis

You now have the basic framework for self-realization. The basics are to ask. Ask for what you really want in life. Commit. Commit to make it happen. Practice. Practice being what you want to become. Surrender. Why are you even trying to do it yourself when you have the most powerful, infinite, orchestrating intelligence in the Universe right at your disposal?

These steps are not sequential. They meld and intermesh together. Each supports the other in your journey. It's a simple model to follow. You'll grow to the degree that you want to grow. Depending on your level of dedication, you'll make exponential leaps very quickly. In fact, you are already realized--always have been, always will be.

A simple picture of the journey to self-realization might look like the diagram on the following page:

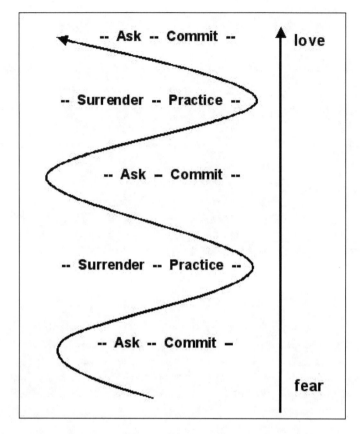

Figure 6. The journey to enlightenment is a progression from fear to love. It is attained by asking, committing, practicing, and surrendering to the Authentic Self within.

You're making a conscious, deliberate journey from living in fear to embodying love. You get to higher states of self-realization through your questions, commitment, practice, and surrender. You keep going, you make progress. You fall back, you learn, you grow. You just keep going. Pretty soon, you're flying up the spiral. When you embark on the inward journey, life soon becomes a joyous, inexplicable, triumphant game.

Now that you know these things, you don't really have to think about them anymore. The framework is an aid to the intellect. It can help you clarify, crystallize, and accelerate different aspects of your evolution. But you don't go around thinking "ask, commit, self-release, self-observation, self-reflection, ask a question, surrender, commitment, etc." any more than you walk around thinking about the blueprint for your own house. You just enjoy living in your house.

Mahatma Gandhi sums up the art of living really well. He writes:

"Keep your thoughts positive because your thoughts become your words.

"Keep your words positive because your words become your behavior.

"Keep your behavior positive because your behavior becomes your habits.

"Keep your habits positive because your habits become your values.

"Keep your values positive because your values become your destiny."

What does it mean to be positive? To have positive words, behavior, habits, values, and destiny? In essence, I think it means to choose things for your life that make you feel good. To do, think, and say things that help make you feel terrific all the time. It's the kind of feeling good that doesn't happen because of positive things occurring around you. Although those external things can be nice, it's a feeling good that emanates from within you. When you're feeling good, you naturally extend that energy outwards and help others experience more goodness too. You focus on being positive, on feeling really good and contributing to the happiness, joy, and well-being of others. This is the art of living.

When it comes to putting it all together, simply focus on how you are feeling. How *are* you feeling, by the way? It's your feelings that guide your transformation. It's your feelings that affirm your self-realization. Are you enlightened? It's really easy to tell. Are you feeling indescribable joy, bliss, and ineffability all the time? Congratulations. You've made it.

There are really only two types of feelings. One type is true positive feeling and the other are false negative emotion. True feelings are positive ones such as bliss, love, truth, oneness, beauty, transcendence, compassion, happiness, inspiration, and appreciation. They are true because they most closely align with reality. Remember, God is perfect, silent, still, whole, creative, life giving, power, and goodness. Therefore, those that most closely align with those characteristics have a sweeter taste of reality about them.

Negative emotions include such things as depression, anxiety, anger, fear, unworthiness, shame, guilt, judgment, condemnation, and apathy. These are all misinterpretations of reality made up by our mind and ego. Therefore, they are false. They occur when we don't get our way. They occur when we try to control things from our small ego-based mind. They feel terrible.

The art of living, then, is to be connected to our true Source all the time, everywhere, and in any situation. Your signal is your feelings. You know you are connected when you simply feel profoundly good all the time. You are happy, joyous, prosperous, healthy, contributing, guided, connected, compassionate, loved, and loving. Good and wonderful things are attracted to you effortlessly. You are without fear, shame, judgment, or condemnation. You experience Oneness and within that Oneness, everything is absolutely grand.

In your day-to-day living, place your attention on those things, people, and ideas that help make you feel great. Choose those things that enliven and inspire you to reveal more truth. Your feelings reveal your inner thought process. Your consistent thoughts form your beliefs. Your beliefs form your attitudes, actions, relationships, activities, and experiences. As you believe, so you are.

The framework identified in this book is one that will take you there. First want enlightenment. Desire it like your head is on fire and God is a bucket of water. Desire starts the process and keeps you in the game. As you desire, continue to ask, commit, practice, and surrender. Just keep on keeping on. This combination guides you to realign your beliefs to more closely match reality and transcend any false and self-limiting beliefs that are preventing you from experiencing it fully. Ask. Commit. Practice. Surrender. Then naturally, by and by, you will shift from being a selfish little clod to become Selfish big clod. You're still selfish because you're still interested in feeling good. You're cultivating a refined sense of Selfishness because it feels better than being selfish. Your sense of Self has expanded to include the entire world and even the entire Universe. You're still a clod because you make plenty of mistakes. You're clumsy, you fall down, and you laugh. You get up and keep doing the best you can with the information and inner resources you have available to you at the time.

To be selfish with a small "s" is to be in a state of fear. You're concerned and consumed with earning, consuming, claiming, and defending. Your inner dialogue follows a similar refrain: "Every day, all day long, I, me, mine." Your only real concern is defending your perception of reality. How can I get ahead? How can I get even? How can I feel more safe and secure? Sure, I want to do good in the world but only after I'm safe and secure myself. First, I'm going to work hard. First I'm going to get the house, wife, car, bank account, status, credibility, recognition, "something," and then I'm going to feel good and then I'm going to do good. Then I'm going to do what I really want to do.

This is selfish. It doesn't feel good. It can't feel good because it's built upon false pretenses. It's a state of fear, repression, and falsity… yuck. You will never, ever arrive with this state of selfishness. It's impossible because it's built from the outside in. You'll never be able to design the outside world to match your inner need for control. Change is a constant. Something will always fall out of alignment. Something will always be there lurking in the dark to take it all away.

To be Selfish, focused on being, serving, contributing, celebrating, appreciating the God within you, everyone and everything, is to be in a state of bliss, joy, and love. Bliss isn't something you earn. It can't be given to you and it can't even be taken away. It just arises naturally out of your true Self-expression. When your sense of Self shifts from "me" to "we," then you naturally experience and express more love and joy. Peace, prosperity, power, and deep satisfaction naturally follow.

My life before waking up was based out of fear. I'd get up early, I'd charge hard. I'd come home irritable. My mind and thoughts were consumed with "how." How will I do this? How will I do that? I spent so much time in my head worrying and fretting about "how" that I was missing my entire life. How will I pay my bills? How can I make more money? How can I get what I want? How, how, how ran my life. I was running so fast and so consumed with "how" that I missed out on the joy, satisfaction, and wonder of every day. I was very forceful and not very powerful. My life then reminds me of a quote from Abd Er-Rahman III of Spain in the year 960 A.D. If it was true over 1,000 years ago, it's even truer now.

> "I have now reigned about 50 years in victory or peace, beloved by my subjects, dreaded by my enemies, and respected by my allies. Riches and honors, power and pleasure, have waited on my call, nor does any earthly blessing appear to have been wanting to my felicity. In this situation, I have diligently numbered the days of pure and

genuine happiness which have fallen to my lot. They amount to 14."

My life after waking up is based on love and contribution and continuing to practice being more real. My presence is very powerful and rarely forceful. It's a total blast. I cry with joy. I'm walking around in a miracle world. I get up each day even earlier in the morning than I used to. The innate need to self-express pours out of me because I can't hold it in. I celebrate who I am and all that I have right now. I read my life's vision and get excited about it. I recommit to my contribution to transform and teach. I identify what cool new creations I want in my life right now. I appreciate all that I am and all that I have. I meditate, pray, and journal. I consciously amp up my frequency for the day ahead because it feels so great to do so. Then throughout my day, my intention is to release anything and everything that is not serving my highest good. I know what it is based upon how I'm feeling.

As I go through my day, fear, judgment, and worry still arise. This is my growth edge. I am usually instantly aware when they do. The feeling is so clear. I get trapped into doing mode. I lose consciousness for a bit. I catch myself, breathe, and reconnect with the bliss within me. Distractions come up. People, situations, and experiences can temporarily overpower my sense of connection. Old habits still arise. My mind is still active, just much calmer than it used to be. I make a little progress every day. If I should notice myself being distracted, I gently bring my attention back to the feeling of reality within. "Thank God for showing me where I am not yet free."

If my life before was all about how-do-I-do-it and forcing things the way I thought they should be, my life today is all about being present and in the flow. My commitment is to focus on what I want and to allow the Universe to orchestrate the how. I am clear about what I want, I return again and again to the presence within me and I am open to the easy way. I seek joy, contribution, effortlessness, happiness, peace, and prosperity.

Usually I'm there. Sometimes I'm not. My old conditioning and constant social pressure of go, go, go, how, how, how, fight, fight, fight, do it, do it, do it can still enter my consciousness. But each time I recommit it gets easier and easier. I know this is where I belong. This is the practice. This is the commitment. Just keep coming back to Source. Find the easy, joyful path. Allow the Universe to orchestrate the details. Enjoy the moment. Live in the present. Yes! Yes!!

Action still happens but it's action from a different kind of place. Life is action. It's always moving. I move along with it. I try not to force it. I focus on what I want and allow it to come to me in the perfect time. I make a commitment to not concern myself with how something shows up. I just focus on being authentic and contributing my passion and gifts. Decisions make themselves. Things get taken care of rapidly. It's all pretty much effortless when I'm connected to my Authentic Self.

When things are happening that I don't particularly enjoy or like, I breathe. I ask myself, "How am I contributing to this situation?" "How can I feel more love and compassion for this person or situation?" I place my attention on what I do want and life unfolds naturally, perfectly, and wonderfully.

When I'm not in touch with how I'm really feeling, the Universe gives me lots and lots of scenarios to point it out.

Just yesterday I was volunteering at the spiritual center. A lady came up to me in a huff. She asked where her water bottle was. My ego felt like she was talking down to me. She was quite rude and condescending. Then right after that, another woman came up and called me "son" and then "Rex."

What the heck is going on here? It felt like everyone around me was being rude and condescending. I thought I was feeling pretty good but the sensations in my being told me to go within and explore deeper. I checked out how I was really feeling on the inside. "What's going on here within me?" I could feel a small split within that I wasn't privy to before. I wasn't feeling totally whole. That's OK. Great lesson. I put my attention on my Authentic Self and as my wholeness increased, life around me shifted. Everybody seemed happy, respectful, and serenely nice again. This shift within me took all of 15 seconds. I'd say a very worthwhile investment of time.

Of course, the Universe sends all kinds of positive things that align with me when I'm feeling connected. Just this morning I was out surfing. Man it was fun! Waves, nature, the sun. I was ecstatic and very conscious of how fun life is. Walking from the beach to my car, three strangers stopped me to talk about guess what? Fun. How fun life is. How much fun it looked like out there. Fun. Life is a mirror and everything you are experiencing is indicative of your beliefs, thoughts, and feelings.

As I go through my day, if negative, false thoughts come up, my commitment is to refuse to give them a place within my consciousness. Instead, I place my attention on what is real within me. The real always instantly transforms what is false.

The objects and events of my outer experience still catch up my ego. Time pressure and that old "how do I do this" pattern continue to creep up on me. This is a tired, deep pattern. When this happens. I might give myself a little internal pep talk, "Oh, there you are again little ego. I see you. I love you. It's all going to be OK." before I place my attention once again on that divine place within that feels so stupendous. The time pressure fades and things take on a vividness and flow. Everything that needs to get completed does but in a miraculous, easy way. Wonderful people, things, and opportunities just come to me naturally. I don't have to fight, force or stretch anything and neither will you.

As I go through my day, I try to make high vibrational choices in foods, relationships, and activities that best support my physical, emotional, and mental well-being. Every so often, I find myself falling off the wagon. I want to pig out, veg out, judge out, fear out, numb out. Each time I go there, I find less and less joy and satisfaction. This is my growth edge. Giving up those things that don't support my highest growth and evolution. At the same time, I don't want to turn back into a rigid machine like I was early in my journey, living from my head and disembodied from my heart. It's a fine balance between living rightly and lightly and giving up hard won ground.

My typical day might look like a series of alpha waves. I start out riding a high. I feel very conscious. I am connected with everyone and everything. I keep that feeling going. Then stuff happens, I get temporarily overwhelmed, and my wave falls off into a trough. I reconnect and ride the wave back up. I go through my day riding the wave and my intention is to be conscious all the time and be open to opportunities to serve.

I consciously choose activities that will bring me joy. If it's not going to bring me joy, I try to put it off until it feels right. In the evening I meditate again and my bliss usually comes back full force. I read in the evening, play with my kids, and flit in and out of pure awareness. I go to sleep feeling so grateful for all of the miraculous things that happened that day. I express deep gratitude for who I am and all that I have right now. I release and forgive others and myself for any perceived hurts and harms. I live and grow and learn each day. This is the journey. This is where questions, commitment, practice, and surrender come in.

It takes courage to live this way. It takes practice. You've surrendered your life to the all-knowing Source within you, which governs, guides, and guards. It tells you what to do, when to act, and how to act. You find yourself in the choiceless choice. You can't rationally explain what it is you are doing. You just know you must do it.

In essence, putting it all together really just means to be loved and loving. To love yourself so completely, so unconditionally that that love transcends and transforms anything false in your life. It feels so good to be you that it hurts. You weep with joy. It's indescribable. As you cultivate love for yourself, you naturally extend that love and compassion to others. You've pierced the veil of separateness and it is grand. Congratulations, you are awakening

Five questions to ponder regarding putting it all together...

1. What does a perfect day look, sound, and feel like to me?

2. What is my growth edge in my transformation?

3. What 10 creations do I want to make manifest in my life right now?

4. What 10 things am I profoundly grateful for?

5. What beliefs am I holding on to that no longer serve me?

I of the Storm

"There's a sense we as humans have kind of peaked. A different way to look at it is it's almost impossible for evolution not to happen."

--Greg Wray

Self-realization is remarkable. It's indescribable. I encourage you to go back for seconds and get some more! But there's another aspect to waking up that we haven't discussed. It's this: HUMANITY MAY DEPEND ON IT.

You can enlighten. You can self-realize. You can transcend any and all self-limiting fears and embody more and more love, acceptance, and power. It is awesome. You have the natural ability to literally raise your frequency to new and previously unknown levels and live life above the fray.

When you commit to the path of awakening, your increasing elevation in consciousness has a positive effect on the entire planet. All is One. It's all connected. As a self-aware person, you are on the cutting edge but you are not alone. Lots and lots of people are beginning to wake up. It's not always easy to be out front. But if you've been called, you already know you don't have much choice in the matter. It's time to step out.

You see, there's something happening now on planet earth that's really shaking things up. A powerful storm is raging. Although it's been developing forever, it has recently begun to radically accelerate its power, force, and scale. It is forecasted to continue to grow and reach a size and range never before witnessed; ripping apart anything and everything not firmly anchored to solid ground. Humanity needs you to be an anchor in this storm and lead the way through its gale for others to follow.

What is this storm? In essence it's that same old storm of change. But this time, the change is bigger, faster, and gnarlier and with major ramifications for the entire planet. My own little microcosm of dealing with change and its repercussions that inspired my self-realization trip is actually a reflection of larger events taking place within the macrocosm. Everything in our world today is undergoing rapid change and the rate of change is accelerating. The consequences of change have bigger implications.

Take a moment and get in touch with the dramatic changes taking place in the world and in your life today. Can you feel the storm occurring? Breathe in the proverbial wind, rain, and the palpable feel of electricity in the air. How do you sense its presence? Is it terrifying or liberating? How will it demonstrate its power in the future? What will life be like once the storm has passed?

My intuition tells me that the dramatic changes occurring in our world today unite to form a fierce storm of transformation. Within this storm's reach swirl cosmic fire, wind, rain, and unimaginable power. The closest analogy I can come up with is that of a hurricane, a series of three expanding and intermeshing rings surrounding a central eye.

The largest, outermost ring is a composition of the many macro-level threats to life as we know it on our small planet.

The speed of this outer ring moves more slowly than the inner rings that drive its turn, but it is picking up steam. In the outer ring reside Earth-wide threats such as climate change, unsustainable resource depletion, the extinction of species, war, potent diseases, fundamentalism, population growth, child poverty, and the imbalance between rich and poor individuals and nations, and other large-scale symptoms of deeper, underlying causes.

The middle ring, smaller but churning faster than the outer one, is formed by our existing local, national, and global man-made systems. Included here are all the organizational structures we've created in an attempt to "manage" the world, our lives, and interactions. Government and non-governmental bodies are found here in all forms and functions to manage the components of our shifting world. Things like natural resources, economic, transportation, legal, religious, political, scientific, police, health care, military, education, arts, entertainment, and social well-being are managed by the systems that we create. These man-made systems can be as large as the United Nations or as small as the corner market. Their common denominator is that they're designed to manage something in the face of change and benefit their stakeholders.

We're beginning to wake up to the fact that most of our man made systems are powerless to manage accelerating change on a global scale. We sense them disintegrating under their own ineffectiveness. The United Nations can seem as powerless to halt the spread of genocide as the corner grocer to compete against Wal-Mart. When big enough change is unleashed, it takes on a life of its own and there's not much, if anything we can do about it. Just as the implosion of an atom creates a powerful bomb, the implosion of these man-made systems causes the outer ring of the storm, the macro-level threats, to gain even greater acceleration and power.

The innermost ring of the storm is the fastest spinning and most fierce. This is the power center that drives the rest of the storm. Here reside billions of human beings contributing to the growth of the storm as well as struggling and striving to make sense of it and manage their lives in the face of it.

There's great turmoil, chaos, and confusion within this inner ring of human beings. It is riddled with strong human emotions of anxiety, anger, guilt, shame, greed and fear. All of the macro changes happening on the outer two rings are actually caused by humanity's collective choices and our seeming inability to stop, pause, or even slow things down to contemplate what we're unleashing. We seem hell bent on a relentless and unstoppable pursuit of technological, biological, economic, and other change with little or no ability to adequately consider, not mentioning manage, the disintegration caused by that change.

From this innermost ring, we can see our collective human consciousness both reflected in the storm and driving and accelerating its momentum. Collectively, we've created a giant cyclone and there's no getting off until the storm peters out or consumes everything in its path. The three intermeshing rings of the storm create a perpetual feedback loop that accelerates the storm's progression. When the outer ring makes one rotation, it causes the inner rings to move faster too. But it's the smallest inner ring that provides the impetus and power to turn.

Every hurricane has a calm and peaceful eye at its center. When there's a real hurricane, the National Oceanic and Atmospheric Administration launches its "Hurricane Hunter" aircraft. These teams of pilots and scientists make a perilous flight through the storm to pierce the eye and gather measurements on its speed, velocity, direction, and more. It must be quite something to fly in the eye of a powerful hurricane. Surrounding your tiny aircraft swirl mighty and destructive forces. But in the eye, it's calm, peaceful, and even tranquil.

Similarly, in this prophetic storm of change, chaos, and disintegration, there's also an eye. If we were to fly through the three outer rings of the storm and reach the safety of the eye, we could take our own measurements and get an entirely new perspective on the storm as well. Fly with me now and let's pierce the eye of the storm together.

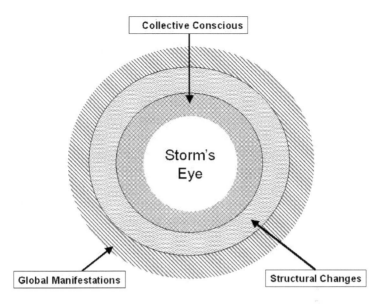

Figure 7. The accelerating change taking place in the world day looks like a three ring hurricane.

The first thing we notice at the eye--surprise, surprise--is laughter, music, and dancing. There are people here! A small group of self-realized people from all walks of life, cultures, and backgrounds. Together we interact with a few of them and although the individuals of this group speak different languages and have diverse customs, it's easy to spot some shared characteristics.

There is a deep sense of authenticity in each person here. Joy, compassion, and acceptance radiate outward and create a palpable feeling of peace and harmony at the center of the storm. Each individual seems to have a deep calling to serve and to contribute to the world. Each expresses themselves creatively and passionately. Mutual respect, trust, learning, and open dialogue are the norm. Love and brotherhood run deep. Knowingness, wisdom, and shared laughter and sadness are common bonds. Beauty, appreciation, and truth are the common currency. In the distance, you can see that more and more people are arriving at the center of the storm each day. Here at the storm's center, you begin to make some very astute observations about the change raging all around.

The first is that storm has a sense of pattern. It is destroying the old, the outdated, and the ineffective. It is cleansing the air, water, and Earth for new ways of thinking, living, and being. There is a purpose to the storm and it is to make space for the new. It is necessary. In order for new structures to take hold, the old ones must implode. From the eye of the storm, this small and growing collective of humanity is both designing and planting the seeds for more enlightened living on our planet. As the storm is causing things to break down it is also creating the space and impetus for new and more coherent, sensible ways of living, being, and interacting to take root. Out of the chaos of the storm a new world that better works for all life is being born. Here at the center, this core and expanding group of self-realized souls is shattering barriers to a brighter and more amazing future than any of us can yet imagine.

In a bolt of insight, you grasp that the transformative change happening in the world today is driven by our collective fragmented consciousness. As individuals we feel fragmented. We perceive ourselves as a physical body. Our actions are driven by fear: fear of death, fear of shame, fear of guilt, fear of losing control. To counteract this fear, we spend a lifetime in strife and struggle. We hoard, we consume, and we try to control. We are attracted to and admire beauty, money, celebrity, sensationalism, and power in a vain attempt to mask or to commiserate with our own inner fears. This fragmented fear-based consciousness not only creates incoherent actions but it also leads to the creation and support of the piecemeal, fragmented, and incoherent systems that are now crumbling across our global society. How can we design and support more coherent, wise, and sensible solutions to the global onslaught of change if it's our fragmented consciousness that creates it in the first place? As Einstein said, you can't solve a problem from the same level of consciousness that created it.

The answer, you realize, is to enlighten. To be more whole, perfect, connected, and sane within your own "I" of the storm. As enough of us make the progression to higher states of living, then the design and deployment of new systems and structures that better work for all life will naturally occur.

The storm of change raging today makes this evolutionary leap both possible and necessary. From the vantage point of the center of the storm, life is joyful, safe, and secure. Here there's a deep resonant call to contribute and help others, who are really just aspects of yourself, into the center so that the insanity stops and the true craziness begins.

What kind of craziness? Oh, I don't know. How about a world that works for everyone. A world where kindness, beauty, and peace are the norm. Where all life is respected. Where everyone has food, a home, and the opportunity to fully contribute their gifts. Where we restore the planetary ecosystem and stop warring, fighting, and pillaging one another. A world where we have fun, get down, and boogie? Like I said, I don't know for certain, but that's a start. Is there an alternative to completely reinventing how we interact, live, and work on our planet? Nope. It should be clear to any thinking person that the current systems and structures in place aren't really serving anybody. In fact, they're downright dangerous to planetary health.

But honestly, although I do care deeply about our planet, humanity, and all life, I don't really care what transitions happen and when. On one hand, it's sad to see suffering, ignorance, and a colossal waste of life occur on our planet. Wouldn't it be nice to just transition out of this era as quickly and with as little suffering as possible? Geez. What a colossal waste. On the other hand, transitions will happen in the perfect way at the perfect time. The truth is that I'm already having a blast here in the center of the storm, hanging out with the rest of my friends on a serious spiritual high. Why don't you join us and contribute your presence and gifts? The more people who join us, the better off we'll all be.

I believe that each of us is alive today to play a role in this evolution. Our purpose is a mighty one and it's a total blast. We are here to enlighten. The chaos and disintegration caused by the storm is freeing up a tremendous amount of energy for human emergence and evolution. There's never been a better time to enlighten. There's never been a more needed time to enlighten and permanently reside in that quiet, expansive, blissful, and all-knowing place within. To become fully alive, aware, contributing, and deeply authentic and transcend chaos and disintegration completely. That sees reality for how it is, for what it is, and laughs.

Five questions to ponder regarding your I of the Storm...

1. What is my role in planetary evolution?

2. How will I contribute my talents and gifts?

3. What positive changes do I see taking shape in the world today?

4. Imagine the world 10 years from now. Miracles have happened. Strange and wonderful things have occurred. What do I see in this new and more perfect world?

5. My life is over. God has written me a letter of sincere appreciation for my contribution in this life. What did God write to me?

Appendix

Summary of the Steps to Awakening

You are already enlightened. Your Authentic Self is you. The journey to enlightenment is to remember what is truly real within you. There are four basic steps to do that: Ask-Commit-Practice-Surrender. These steps are not sequential. They blend and intermesh as you evolve. But wherever you are in your progression you must desire lasting freedom more than you desire anything else.

Ask

Ask yourself the most important questions of your own life. You already have all the answers. They reside within your own heart. The more you ask, the more frequent and clearer your inner responses become. You possess the perfect onboard guidance system that both sends and receives exactly what you ask for. So ask.

Commit

The spiritual journey takes great commitment. You will be tested. It's OK. The trials simply reveal your inner strength. You will accomplish great things by your dedication. Whatever trials should emerge just keep on keeping on and you will one day be triumphant.

Practice

Practice every day all day long. Be self-responsible and self-observant in your relationships and interactions. Regularly meditate, pray, and self-reflect on the light of reality within you. Take time out from the day-to-day and allow yourself to release those things that no longer serve your highest good. Get support. Ask for help. Be open to receive. The higher you go, the more you practice.

Surrender

Surrender is the ultimate practice. Turn everything in your life over to your Authentic Self. Allow it to orchestrate all the details for your greatest good. Release. Let go. Allow love to consume you entirely. Remember that you are a pure being of divine love, light, and authentic self-expression; so if you should happen to be struggling, get out of your own way by surrendering to what's real within you.

Review of Key Questions

Five questions to ponder regarding your call to transformation...

1. What's working really well in my life? What's not working so well?

2. What are the subtle, and not so subtle signs, pointing to potential disintegration?

3. If I could snap my fingers and transform anything in my life instantly, what would it be, what would I change?

4. Earlier in my life I experienced a call to transform. To take a new direction, go a new route, or discover something new about myself. When was it? What happened as a result? What were the ultimate benefits?

5. Who do I know who has totally transformed themselves from the inside out? What was their experience? How does it relate to my own?

Five questions to ponder regarding your experience of enlightenment...

1. What is my most memorable transcendent, peak experience – my awakening, perhaps shocking, and out-of-mind experience? When did it occur?

2. Do I want to spend more time in this realm today? Is there anything scary or threatening about it?

3. Whom do I know, personally or from afar, who exemplifies an enlightened being? What do I think their life is like?

4. What does my rationale mind think about enlightenment? If I imagine myself as fully enlightened, do any inner judgments, fears, or criticisms arise?

5. What is my vision of my life at its highest potential? My ultimate vision -- as good as it gets.

Five questions to ponder regarding your life's questions...

1. Can I realize myself fully in this lifetime? Do I even want to? Why or why not?

2. Am I ready for enlightenment? Why or why not?

3. What question, or questions, do I choose for myself that will lead my life in the direction I want to go?

4. I wonder what unconscious questions, doubts, fears, and negative beliefs may be contributing to my current condition?

5. *Why* do I do what I do? *Why* am I the way I am?

Five questions to ponder regarding your commitment to enlightenment...

1. What is my highest goal in life?

2. How committed am I to my enlightenment?

3. How do I demonstrate this commitment today?

4. How can I demonstrate it more fully?

5. What other commitments have I chosen that keep me from being fully self-realized?

Five questions to ponder regarding your practice...

1. What are my current spiritual practices? How are they serving me? Are any not serving me?

2. How responsible am I being with my life?

3. How observant am I of my thoughts and feelings? How do I know when I'm connected and when I'm not?

4. What do I need to release from my life? What do I need to accept and embrace?

5. What support will help me get to where I really want to be?

Five questions to ponder regarding your surrender...

1. Who or what is God? Is it safe to surrender to God?

2. What aspects of my life am I still trying to control?

3. What am I willing to give up in order to have enlightenment?

4. How does God reveal itself in my life today?

5. What fears keep me from surrendering completely?

Five questions to ponder regarding putting it all together…

1. What does a perfect day look, sound, and feel like to me?

2. What is my growth edge in my transformation?

3. What 10 creations do I want to make manifest in my life right now?

4. What 10 things am I profoundly grateful for?

5. What beliefs am I holding on to that no longer serve me?

Five questions to ponder regarding your I of the Storm…

1. What is my role in planetary evolution?

2. How will I contribute my talents and gifts?

3. What positive changes do I see taking shape in the world today?

4. Imagine the world 10 years from now. Miracles have happened. Strange and wonderful things have occurred. What do I see in this new and more perfect world?

Appendix

5. My life is over. God has written me a letter of sincere appreciation for my contribution in this life. What did God write to me?

Resources for Your Trip

Below is a list of resources for spirit-mind-body that I've personally experienced and found valuable. I recognize that there's lots of great stuff out there that I haven't yet explored. But these resources all helped me tremendously at various points along the way. So in the spirit of sharing, explore and enjoy. Also, please submit your own valued resources at http://www.lexsisney.com.

Workshops

I think the role of a workshop is to provide an immersive experience where you can go deep and discover. Peer-to-peer learning and exchange provides priceless benefits as well.

Adizes Institute

If you're in business then you should know about the Adizes methodology. It's a suite of time-tested protocols that you can apply within your organization to accelerate change and create environments for human emergence. Learn more at http://www.adizes.com.

Chopra Center

The Chopra Center in Carlsbad, Calif. regularly host mind-body retreats in various locations around the globe. I've done several with them and have always had a transformative experience. Learn more at http://www.chopra.com.

Esalen

Perhaps the birthplace of the modern day human potential movement, Esalen hosts a wide variety of personal and spiritual development workshops in magical Big Sur. Famous for their ocean view natural hot springs and organic cuisine, it's a one-of-a-kind place. Learn more at http://www.esalen.com

Heart Math

Heart Math is the world's foremost authority on the role of the heart in human transformation. It's very powerful and practical stuff to unleash creativity, reduce stress, and improve overall well being. Learn more at http://www.heartmath.com.

Hendricks Institute
Do you want to have more fun in your life, enjoy more conscious loving relationships, and express your true genius? If so, then spend some time at a Hendricks event. Learn more at http://www.hendricks.com.

Hoffman Institute
The Hoffman Quadrinity Process provides extraordinary experiences for adults who are looking for transformational changes in their lives. I got my first taste of my Authentic Self through this process as have many, many others. Learn more at http://www.hoffmaninstitute.org.

IMAGO Relationship Therapy
Executive director Rick Brown hosts a really phenomenal couples workshop at various locations around the country. Learn more at http://www.rickbrown.org.

Institute of Noetic Sciences
If you have a love for quantum physics and modern science, then you absolutely must acquaint yourself with the Institute of Noetic Sciences in Napa, Calif. Founded by former Apollo Astronaut Edgar Mitchell, IONS regularly hosts cutting edge workshops. Learn more at http://www.ions.org.

Science of Mind
I have to admit that the name sounds a little too orthodox but the content from Science of Mind is pure practical wisdom. If you want to master the Law of Attraction, learn how to pray, or participate in a trans-denominational spiritual community, then you might find what you're looking for here. Learn more at http://www.religiousscience.org, http://www.agapelive.com, or http://www.centeroftheheart.com.

Self Awareness Institute

The Self Awareness Institute hosts virtual classes on meditation and self-awakening. It's very powerful and transformative stuff from the convenience of your telephone. Learn more at http://www.selfawareness.com.

Spiral Dynamics

If you want to better understand why humans do what they do and how to orchestrate positive social shifts, take a workshop from the Spiral Dynamics Institute. Learn more at http://www.spiraldynamics.org.

Usui Reiki

I think everyone should know hands on energy healing as part of their household medicine cabinet. Reiki is easy to learn and completely safe. It's yet another method to connect with Source energy and to transmit it through the hands, to yourself and others, creating the space for improved health and enhanced quality of life. During Reiki classes, students experience the techniques first hand. I'm told that Reiki's use around the world and in hospitals and medical centers continues to grow. The gift of self-healing and healing others is priceless. http://www.usuireikicenter.org.

White Lotus Yoga Center

Visit this fun and beautiful setting led by master yogis. I took a pranayama breathing course from White Lotus years ago and still use the techniques today. Learn more at http://www.whitelotus.org

Media

There's wonderful media available to augment your journey, inspire and uplift. Here are some of my favorites.

Appendix

Magazines

Ode
The tag line for Ode reads "for intelligent optimists." This is just a great magazine covering a wide array of global issues. If you're ever feeling down about the state of the world, read Ode and change your perspective. Learn more at http://www.odemagazine.com.

Shift
The magazine of the Institute of Noetic Sciences does a good job of covering the latest in quantum physics, mind-body healing, while blending ancient wisdom with modern science. http://www.ions.org.

What is Enlightenment?
Read What is Enlightenment? for cutting edge perspectives on spirituality in an evolving world. Learn more at http://www.wie.org.

Film

Humanity Ascending
Check out this new documentary series from philosopher and futurist Barbara Marx Hubbard for a deeper understanding of this evolving, transformative time humanity is moving through. http://www.barbaramarxhubbard.com.

Spiritual Cinema Circle
Get an inspiring collection of spiritually themed movies in your mailbox each month. They remind me of how cool it is to be a human being. Visit http://www.spiritualcinemacircle.com

The Secret
The Secret is a fun video on the Law of Attraction. I love how new spins on ancient wisdom continue to pour out. Check out http://www.thesecret.tv.

What the Bleep Do We Know?

A pop-culture hit that captures the essence of "as within-so without" living. Includes great explanations from leading quantum physicists. Learn more at http://www.whatthebleep.com.

Audio & Music

There's so much good music out there that promotes healing and deeper states of consciousness that I can't even make a recommendation other than to follow your heart.

Sounds True

Sounds True has a large and growing collection of conscious themed audio books and music. You can pay them a visit at http://www.soundstrue.com

Healing & Release

A big part of the journey to self-realization is to clear out the physical and subtle gunk that is clogging your connection to Source. In addition to surrounding yourself with natural air, water, light, and materials, as well as consuming vibrant, healthy foods, here are some of my favorite resources to help with that clearing process on a physical level.

American Health Institute

Everyone needs a talented local holistic healer, but if you live or travel in the Los Angeles or Santa Barbara region, pay a visit to the American Health Institute. Led by Dr. Michael Galitzer the American Health Institute specializes in anti-aging, bio-identical hormone replacement, and homeopathics. Dr. Galitzer is featured in several best selling books including Alternative Medicine: The Definitive Guide (great book by the way). Learn more at http://www.ahealth.com/.

Detox

Regular detoxification is a good thing. My favorite method of detoxification and internal cleansing is the Master Cleanse, also called the Lemonade Diet. It's simple, cheap and very effective. Learn more at http://therawfoodsite.com/mastercleanse.htm.

Esoteric Acupuncture

Esoteric Acupuncture is a relatively new form of acupuncture that combines traditional acupuncture with sacred geometry, chakra balancing, and other ancient traditions. It's designed for people who are already in good health and actively engaged in their own spiritual practices and development. Learn more at http://esotericacupuncture.blogspot.com/.

Far Infrared Sauna

Every great wisdom tradition involves heat to transform the body-mind. My favorite way to start the day after meditation is to take a far-infrared sauna. It feels awesome (and I don't even like saunas). Far infrared is an invisible spectrum of light that warms objects without warming the air between the source and the object. For example, 80% of the sun's rays are infrared. The heat goes deep, you sweat a lot, and it feels fantastic. There are many purported health benefits of far infrared as well. I use a model from Sundance Sauna at http://www.sundancesauna.com and they have great customer service.

Rolfing

Rolfing realigns your physical structure so that its better integrated in gravity. Research has demonstrated that Rolfing creates a more efficient use of the muscles, allows the body to conserve energy, and creates more economical and refined patterns of movement. I've noticed lasting changes in my posture from the practice. Find out more at http://www.rolf.org.

Q2 Energy Spa

Created in Australia, this little device sits with you in a tub of water and recharges your biological battery. I can't speak for the science but I can tell you that it *feels* like it does just that. Learn more at http://www.q2.com.au/.

Coaching

A coach is a personal choice. My number one suggestion is to find a coach who is walking the talk. That is, if you want more money, find a coach who makes a lot of money. If you want more spirituality, find a coach who embodies spirituality, etc. I also encourage you to find a coach who sees the world a little bit differently than you do. There's an old adage that if two people agree, one of them is unnecessary. Flat out: coaching really works. I encourage you to try it. Location doesn't matter. Telephone coaching is just as impactful as in-person coaching. Here are two coaches that helped me tremendously at various times:

Euphrasia Carroll

Euphrasia Carroll is a specialist in heart intelligence. She absolutely helped me to access more intuition and creativity directly from my heart. Visit Euphrasia at http://www.easebalanceclarity.com.

Lindsay Wagner

Lindsay Wagner is a specialist on authentic leadership. She really helped me to cultivate compassion and empathy for myself when I most needed it. Visit Lindsay at http://www.authenticore.com.

You can find additional coaches at http://www.findacoach.com/index.html

References and Further Reading

Adizes, Ichak. *Managing Corporate Lifecycles;* The Adizes Institute Publishing, 2004

Beck, Don et al, Spiral Dynamics: Mastering Values, Leadership and Change; *Blackwell Publishing Professional, 1996.*

Berry, Thomas, The Great Work; Random House, 1990

Bloom, Howard, Global Brain: The Evolution of Mass Mind from the Big Bang to the 21st Century; Wiley, 2001

Bloom, Howard K., The Lucifer Principle; Atlantic Monthly Press, 1997
Bohm, David and Basil J. Hiley, *The Undivided Universe*; Routledge, 1993

Brown, Lester R., *Plan B: Rescuing a Planet Under Stress and a Civilization In Trouble*; Earth Policy Institute, 2003

Butterworth, Eric, *Spiritual Economics: The Principles and Process of True Prosperity*; Unity Books, 2001

Childre, Doc Lew and Howard Martin, *The HeartMath Solution*; Harper Collins, 1999

Chopra, Deepak, *How to Know God: The Soul's Journey Into the Mystery of Mysteries*; Harmony Books, 2000

Chopra, Deepak, *The Seven Spiritual Laws of Success*; New World Library/Amber-Allen Publishing, 1994

Das, Lama Surya, *Awakening to the Sacred*; Broadway, 1999

de Mello, Anthony, *Awareness*; Double Day, 1990

Gerber, Richard, M.D., Vibrational Medicine; Bear & Co., 2001
Gladwell, Malcolm, *The Tipping Point*; Back Bay Books, 2002

Greene, Brian, The Elegant Universe; W.W. Norton & Co., 2003

Haich, Elisabeth and Selvarajan Yesudian, *Sexual Energy and Yoga*; Aurora Press, 1982

Harman, Willis, *Global Mind Change*; Berrett-Koehler Publishers, 1998

Harman, Willis et al, *Creative Work*; World Business Academy, 1990

Hartranft, Chip, *The Yoga-Sutra of Pantanjali*, Shambhala, 2003

Hartzell, Mary and Daniel Siegel, M.D., Parenting From the Inside Out; Putnam, 2003

Hawken, Paul, *The Ecology of Commerce*; Harper Collins, 1994

Hawkins, David, M.D., *Power vs. Force: An Anatomy of Consciousness*, Veritas Publishing, 1995

Hendricks, Gay and Kate Ludeman, *The Corporate Mystic: A Guidebook for Visionaries with Their Feet on the Ground*; Bantam, 1997

Hendricks, Gay, *The Ten-Second Miracle: Creating Relationship Breakthroughs*; HarperSanFrancisco, 1998

Hicks, Esther and Jerry Hicks, *Ask and It is Given: Learning to Manifest Your Desires*; Hay House, 2004

Holmes, Ernest, *Living the Science of Mind*; DeVorss & Co., 1999

Holmes, Ernest, *Love and Law*; United Church of Religious Science, 1994

Holmes, Ernest, *The Science of Mind*; Tarcher, 1998

Hubbard, Barbara Marx, *Conscious Evolution*; New World Library, 1998

Jones, Laurie Beth, *The Path: Creating Your Mission Statement for Work and Life*; Hyperion, 1996

Kurzweil, Ray, *The Singularity Is Near*; Penguin Group, 2006

Landsberg, Max, *The Tao of Coaching*, Profile Books Limited, 2005

Maharaj, Nisargadatta, I Am That; Acorn Press, 1973 Reprint edition from 1990

Maslow, Abraham H., *Religions, Values, and Peak-Experiences*; Penguin, 1994

Maslow, A.H., *The Farthest Regions of Human Nature*; Penguin, 1970

McTaggart, Lynne, *The Field*; Harper Collins, 2003

May, Gerald, M.D., *Will and Spirit*; Harper Collins, 1982

Osho, *Awareness, The Key to Living in Balance*; Osho International, 2001

Proctor, Bob, *You Were Born Rich*; LifeSuccess Productions, 1997

Ray, Paul and Sherry Ruth Anderson, The Cultural Creatives; Three Rivers Press, 2001

Russell, Peter, *The Global Brain Awakens*; Global Brain Inc., 1995

Sankey, Mikio, Ph.D, *Esoteric Acupuncture: Gateway to Expanded Healing*; Mountain Castle Publishing, 1999

Sinetar, Marsha, Do What You Love, The Money Will Follow; Dell, 1989

Stiles, Mukunda, Yoga Sutras of Pantanjali; Wieser Books, 2002

Talbot, Michael, *Mysticism and the New Physics*; Penguin, 1993

Talbot, Michael, The Holographic Universe; Harper Collins, 1991

Tolle, Eckhart, *The Power of Now*; New World Library, 1999

Toms, Michael and Justine Toms, True Work: Doing What You Love and Loving What You Do, Bell Tower, 1998

Walsh, Roger, M.D., *Essential Spirituality*; Wiley, 1999

Wilber, Ken, *A Theory of Everything*; Shambhala, 2001

Wolcott, William et al, *The Metabolic Typing Diet*; Broadway Books, 2000

Zohar, Danah and Ian Marshall, Spiritual Capital: Wealth We Can Live By; Berrett-Koehler Publishers, 2004

About the Author

Lex Sisney's mission is to transform himself from the inside out and share his progression along the way. Surrendering his life to a simple ideal "transform and teach" Lex guides fellow entrepreneurs and business leaders to lasting clarity, prosperity, and peace of mind.

When Lex was in his early thirties he had a life-changing epiphany. As Lex puts it, "Struggling to manage the explosive growth of my high-tech company as well as my marriage, baby daughter, new home, and my health and sanity, it felt like my life was imploding.

Depressed and frustrated, I realized that everything I had learned about managing my life, my family, and my business wasn't enough in the face of accelerating change. I was trying to manage my life from the outside-in, striving to make it, do it, force it and 'arrive.'

My life was successful on the surface but beneath a cool and calm veneer, I could feel everything I care deeply about slowly disintegrating. Like a leaky pipe that doesn't reveal its fissures until the water pressure is severe, it took a rapid amount of change in my life to reveal the cracks in the methods that originally brought me success."

This epiphany led Lex on a remarkable journey to discover new and better methods to successfully manage a life, a career, and a business. Collectively, these methods represent an entirely new way of living and working, one that flows consciously from inside the Self and out into the world. Called Authentic Self Leadership, it's the knowledge, commitment and practice of learning to develop and turn life over completely to the Authentic Self.

Today, Lex is an expert at developing Authentic Self Leadership in individuals and organizations. He has been certified in several next generation change management philosophies including the Adizes® methodology, Spiral Dynamics®, HeartMath® and numerous other modalities.

Lex's career is defined by a series of firsts: Lex designed two of the world's first electronic procurement services, the first integrated distance learning/personal coaching network, as well as the first aggregate affiliate marketing network. With Lex as CEO and Chairman, the latter grew to become the world's largest company of its type and was acquired in 2003.

Lex has served in leadership roles in the Young Presidents Organization (Santa Barbara Chapter) and the American Marketing Association (University of St. Thomas) blowing the roof off new membership recruitment. An avid reader, author, dynamic thinker, coach, and lecturer, Lex brings his wisdom, passion, presence and insight into all his client activities.

Most dearly, Lex is married to a remarkable woman, Shanna Sisney, who is the catalyst for his personal growth and continued expansion. They live and play in Santa Barbara, CA with their children Alexa and Reid who, not coincidentally, are Lex and Shanna's greatest teachers.

Made in United States
Orlando, FL
28 July 2024

49631459R00114